LILA RAICEK

Lila Raicek is a New York-based playwright and screenwriter making her West End debut with *My Master Builder*. In theatre, her new plays include *Fire Season*, inspired by *Measure for Measure*, in pre-production; and *Tulla,* about painter Edvard Munch, for Seaview Productions. Her play *Vertebrae* (New York Theatre Workshop) was awarded the Araca Group's Graduate Playwriting Award, and *Love Lab* received the inaugural Clifford Odets Ensemble Play Commission. In television, she has created original series and adapted bestselling books for Fifth Season, Netflix, Paramount, and wrote on *Younger* and *Gossip Girl*. Her debut novel *The Plunge* will be published in 2026 by HarperCollins. She holds an MFA in Playwriting from Columbia University and a BA summa cum laude in Creative Writing from Barnard College, Columbia University.

Other Titles in this Series

Annie Baker
THE ANTIPODES
THE FLICK
INFINITE LIFE
JOHN

Chris Bush
THE ASSASSINATION OF KATIE HOPKINS
THE CHANGING ROOM
CHRIS BUSH PLAYS: ONE
A DOLL'S HOUSE *after* Ibsen
FAUSTUS: THAT DAMNED WOMAN
HUNGRY
JANE EYRE *after* Brontë
THE LAST NOËL
OTHERLAND
ROBIN HOOD AND THE
   CHRISTMAS HEIST
ROCK / PAPER / SCISSORS
STANDING AT THE SKY'S EDGE
   with Richard Hawley
STEEL

Jez Butterworth
THE FERRYMAN
THE HILLS OF CALIFORNIA
JERUSALEM
JEZ BUTTERWORTH PLAYS: ONE
JEZ BUTTERWORTH PLAYS: TWO
MOJO
THE NIGHT HERON
PARLOUR SONG
THE RIVER
THE WINTERLING

Caryl Churchill
BLUE HEART
CHURCHILL PLAYS: THREE
CHURCHILL PLAYS: FOUR
CHURCHILL PLAYS: FIVE
CHURCHILL: SHORTS
CLOUD NINE
DING DONG THE WICKED
A DREAM PLAY *after* Strindberg
DRUNK ENOUGH TO SAY I LOVE YOU?
ESCAPED ALONE
FAR AWAY
GLASS. KILL. BLUEBEARD'S FRIENDS.
   IMP.
HERE WE GO
HOTEL
ICECREAM
LIGHT SHINING IN
   BUCKINGHAMSHIRE
LOVE AND INFORMATION
MAD FOREST
A NUMBER
PIGS AND DOGS
SEVEN JEWISH CHILDREN
THE SKRIKER
THIS IS A CHAIR
THYESTES *after* Seneca
TRAPS
WHAT IF IF ONLY

Lindsey Ferrentino
THE FEAR OF 13
UGLY LIES THE BONE

Jeremy O. Harris
'DADDY': A MELODRAMA
SLAVE PLAY

Natasha Gordon
NINE NIGHT

Branden Jacobs-Jenkins
APPROPRIATE
THE COMEUPPANCE
GLORIA
AN OCTOROON

Lucy Kirkwood
BEAUTY AND THE BEAST
   with Katie Mitchell
BLOODY WIMMIN
THE CHILDREN
CHIMERICA
HEDDA *after* Ibsen
THE HUMAN BODY
IT FELT EMPTY WHEN THE HEART
   WENT AT FIRST BUT IT IS
   ALRIGHT NOW
LUCY KIRKWOOD PLAYS: ONE
MOSQUITOES
NSFW
RAPTURE
TINDERBOX
THE WELKIN

Tony Kushner
ANGELS IN AMERICA –
   PARTS ONE AND TWO
CAROLINE, OR CHANGE
HOMEBODY/KABUL
THE VISIT, OR THE OLD LADY
   COMES TO CALL
   after Friedrich Dürrenmatt

Kimber Lee
UNTITLED F*CK M*SS S**GON PLAY

Lynn Nottage
CLYDE'S
CRUMBS FROM THE TABLE OF JOY
INTIMATE APPAREL
MLIMA'S TALE
RUINED
SWEAT

Mark Rosenblatt
GIANT

Jack Thorne
2ND MAY 1997
AFTER LIFE
BUNNY
BURYING YOUR BROTHER IN
   THE PAVEMENT
A CHRISTMAS CAROL *after* Dickens
THE END OF HISTORY…
HOPE
JACK THORNE PLAYS: ONE
JACK THORNE PLAYS: TWO
JUNKYARD
LET THE RIGHT ONE IN
   after John Ajvide Lindqvist
THE MOTIVE AND THE CUE
MYDIDAE
THE SOLID LIFE OF SUGAR WATER
STACY & FANNY AND FAGGOT
WHEN YOU CURE ME
WHEN WINSTON WENT TO WAR WITH
   THE WIRELESS
WOYZECK *after* Büchner

debbie tucker green
BORN BAD
DEBBIE TUCKER GREEN PLAYS: ONE
DIRTY BUTTERFLY
EAR FOR EYE
HANG
NUT
A PROFOUNDLY AFFECTIONATE,
   PASSIONATE DEVOTION TO
   SOMEONE (– *NOUN*)
RANDOM
STONING MARY
TRADE & GENERATIONS
TRUTH AND RECONCILIATION

Phoebe Waller-Bridge
FLEABAG

Lila Raicek

MY MASTER BUILDER

NICK HERN BOOKS
London
www.nickhernbooks.co.uk

A Nick Hern Book

My Master Builder first published in Great Britain as a paperback original in 2025 by Nick Hern Books Limited, The Glasshouse, 49a Goldhawk Road, London W12 8QP

My Master Builder copyright © 2025 Lila Raicek

Lila Raicek has asserted her right to be identified as the author of this work

Cover: design:**feast**creative.com
Photography: Oliver Rosser & Steven Simko

Typeset and designed by Nick Hern Books, London
Printed in Great Britain by Mimeo Ltd, Huntingdon, Cambridgeshire PE29 6XX

A CIP catalogue record for this book is available from the British Library

ISBN   978 1 83904 460 1

CAUTION   All rights whatsoever in this play are strictly reserved. Requests to reproduce the text in whole or in part should be addressed to the publisher. This book may not be used, in whole or in part, for the development or training of artificial intelligence technologies or systems.

Performing Rights   Applications for performance, including readings and excerpts, throughout the world should be addressed to Creative Artists Agency, 405 Lexington Avenue, 19th Floor, New York City, NY 10174, USA, *fax* +1 (212) 277 9099, *email* olivier.sultan@caa.com

No performance of any kind may be given unless a licence has been obtained. Applications should be made before rehearsals begin. Publication of this play does not necessarily indicate its availability for performance.

www.nickhernbooks.co.uk/environmental-policy

Nick Hern Books' authorised representative in the EU is
Easy Access System Europe – Mustamäe tee 50, 10621 Tallinn, Estonia
email gpsr.requests@easproject.com

My Master Builder was first performed at Wyndham's Theatre, London, on 29 April 2025 (previews from 17 April), presented by Marketstall, MGC and Seaview, with the following cast:

HENRY SOLNESS	Ewan McGregor
MATHILDE	Elizabeth Debicki
ELENA SOLNESS	Kate Fleetwood
RAGNAR	David Ajala
KAIA	Mirren Mack

UNDERSTUDIES

RAGNAR	Kai Antoine
HENRY SOLNESS	Richard Ede
ELENA SOLNESS	Elizabeth Healey
MATHILDE/KAIA	Jane Mahady

SUPERNUMERARIES
Jeremy Booth
Emilio Cavaciuti
Maxwell Chartey
Sophie Kean
Drew Paterson
Jolyon Young

Director	Michael Grandage
Set and Costume Designer	Richard Kent
Lighting Designer	Paule Constable
Sound Designer and Composer	Adam Cork
Casting Director	Sophie Holland CSA
Movement and Intimacy Coordinator	Ben Wright
Associate Director	Bethany West

Production Manager	Kate West
Props Supervisor	Kate Margretts
Costume Supervisor	Lisa Aitken
Hair & Make-up Supervisor	Gilly Church
Company Stage Manager	Greg Shimmin
Deputy Stage Manager	Lucy Bradford
Assistant Stage Manager	Christopher Carr
Head of Wardrobe	Maria Maguire
Wardrobe Deputy	Linski Kilcourse
Wardrobe Assistant	Genieve Vasconcelos
Principal Dresser	Verity Dupont
Hair & Make-up	Lauren Osborne
Sound No. 1	James Scotney
Sound No. 2	Amber Carey

'She often seemed like a little bird of prey, who would gladly have included me among her victims... She did not get hold of me, but I got hold of her – for my play.'

Henrik Ibsen, on Emilie Bardach (1891)

'And why not a bird of prey! Why shouldn't I go hunting too? Take the prey I want? If I can get my claws into it, and hold it firm.'

Hilde, The Master Builder (*1892*)

Characters

HENRY SOLNESS, *fifties, British, architect and academic*
ELENA SOLNESS, *fifties, British, publishing executive*
MATHILDE, *thirty, American, writer*
RAGNAR, *forty, British-African, rising architect*
KAIA, *thirty, American, Elena's editorial assistant*

Setting

July 4th. The Hamptons, New York.

The chapel can be seen as both real and abstract, bending the spatial reality of the play. Part memorial pavilion, part spiritual sanctuary. A sculptural pyramid-shape of translucent blocks, with perforated slats that allow a play of light and shadow. It rises towards a soaring spire, reflecting the sky beyond.

Each time the chapel is revealed, it should subtly shapeshift: the color, the angle, the light.

Note

My Master Builder was inspired by Henrik Ibsen's *The Master Builder (Bygmester Solness)*, his autobiographical play published in 1892.

In the last line of his play, Hilda cries out: 'My – my master builder! Mine!'

This text went to press before the end of rehearsals and so may differ slightly from the play as performed.

ACT ONE

Scene One

A sunlit afternoon in The Hamptons. Bucolic green acres stretching towards the blue sea.

On the edge of a field, a breathtaking vertical structure ascends: the CHAPEL.

HENRY SOLNESS, *British, stands before his new work. A commanding, charismatic visionary with an intensely poetic soul.*

Ahead of the unveiling, later that evening, he is being filmed for a press segment on the CHAPEL, *in his most impassioned, captivating element:*

HENRY. The thing about being an architect is you have this transformative, almost *transcendent* power to turn dreams into reality, with brick and mortar, and to turn history into hope. Architecture is the fiction of the real world, if you think about it, which is completely *insane* – and why architects get a bad rap, they all think they're bloody Howard Roark. But it's the reason memory remains the key to all of my work: memory is the foundation that grounds it with *meaning*, that connects the past to the future. Even our most problematic, or tragic ruins – such as the site we're standing on now – carry memories that demand our attention, our preservation, that remind us where we have come from and what we have survived.

Beat.

When I was envisioning how to reconstruct this nineteenth-century old Whaler's Church – after it was destroyed in a devastating fire – the intention was to honor its character as a space of contemplation, yet one for our creative soul. I wanted it to be like… the David Bowie of chapels! On that slippery edge between the sacred and the profane…

Excitedly, HENRY *scales the exterior of the* CHAPEL, *pausing on a low landing.*

And the best part is: it can be climbed! Well, before that feature was banned by some gormless committee. But still, the chapel was built to be *ascended* – so anyone, at anytime, can feel they are reaching closer to the stars.

HENRY *jumps down as 'Moonage Daydream' by David Bowie plays.*

The CHAPEL *recedes.*

Lights up on:

Scene Two

Later that day.

An atrium in a modern house. A fluid indoor-outdoor space, light-filled and inviting. Beyond, the dunes, and the sea glimmering in the distance.

ELENA SOLNESS, *British, a magnetic powerhouse at the top of the publishing industry, arranges a stack of place cards ahead of dinner this evening. She moves them like a chess master, but something is off.*

ELENA. No.

Beat, moves a card.

No.

Beat, moves a card.

…maybe?

Beat, moves a card.

No.

ELENA *picks up another card. As she is about to move it, she stops.*

She stares at the name on the card. Deeply unsettled by it.

KAIA, *thirty, American, her editorial assistant, enters.*

KAIA. The permit for the fireworks is all set.

ELENA *quickly places the card down.*

ELENA. Oh brilliant. How did you manage to pull it off?

KAIA. I said you'd write a scathing exposé on bribery in the Southampton fire department.

ELENA. Clever girl. Bravo!

KAIA. Learned from the best.

ELENA. And you know I'd print it, too.

ELENA *picks up another card.*

KAIA. Is everything okay?

ELENA. Hmmm? Yes, of course. Why?

KAIA. It's just… you hate seating arrangements.

ELENA. True. They should be *illegal*, really.

KAIA. And I've only seen you use them once…

ELENA. Right… at Henry's fiftieth. I placed my seat beside his nemesis, hoping Henry might protest, cause a scene…

Beat.

But he didn't.

KAIA. I recall. So…

ELENA. So, why not stir up a little drama tonight! God knows we can't take another dinner of crusty old men wanking on about who's *erected* the biggest tower.

KAIA *picks up a card.*

KAIA. Oh no, that art-collector guy is coming?

ELENA. Ghastly, I know. But I'm hoping he'll hire Henry for the renovation of his new art foundation.

KAIA. Should we put them next to each other then?

ELENA. No, better not. Shall we put him next to you?

KAIA. Oh no no, please don't, he'll try to maul me like last time –

ELENA. *Maul* you? With those prehistoric teeth of his?

ELENA plucks the card from KAIA, and switches it with another card on the table.

There! He can maul the Director of the Met instead.

KAIA. Oh I forgot – he called to say he's stuck in traffic.

ELENA. Good, he's a little *prick* for not giving Henry the commission for their annex.

KAIA. Also, your attorney called...?

ELENA. Don't tell me I accidentally invited him too.

KAIA. No, he called to say the 'papers' were almost ready.

Beat. ELENA *takes this in, distressed.*

ELENA. Well, talk about opportune timing.

KAIA. Is it?

ELENA. Depending on if I serve them, I suppose.

Beat.

KAIA. Elena, I had no idea. You didn't tell me – ?

ELENA. I haven't told anyone. Not even my own husband.

KAIA. But – but you've been married nearly twenty years.

ELENA. Correct. And?

KAIA. I just thought you two were still so...

ELENA.... what?

KAIA. I don't know. Still in love.

ELENA. *Love...*

Beat.

The thing is, Kaia, somehow, somewhere in marriage, the wires of love and pain become so crossed through the years that you cannot tell one from the other. And the only way to unravel them, to untangle yourself from the wreck is to cut yourself free.

Beat. Then ELENA *turns back to the business of place cards, diverting her energy.*

Right. So which guest shall *I* maul tonight?

KAIA. Elena, are you okay?

ELENA. Kaia, darling, I've never felt better.

Beat.

As someone once said, the chains of marriage are so heavy that it takes two to bear them – and sometimes <u>three</u>.

ELENA *checks her phone.*

Have you heard from Ragnar yet?

KAIA. Yes, he said his ETA is any moment now.

ELENA. What?! Why didn't you tell me?

KAIA. I thought you knew – !

ELENA. He texted *you*?!

KAIA. You asked me to be in touch with directions!

ELENA *anxiously checks herself.*

ELENA. Oh god, I haven't even showered yet. How do I look?

KAIA. Stunning.

ELENA. I'll <u>fire</u> you if you're lying to me.

KAIA. That's why I'm not.

Beat. ELENA *turns to* KAIA *in a moment of insecurity.*

ELENA. Kaia, be honest with me. Do you think a *younger* man like Ragnar could ever be... you know, interested?

KAIA. How could anyone not be?

ELENA. I don't know. I suppose the last time I was single was when I was about your age...

Beat.

A terrifying thought.

KAIA. Don't they say age is just a number?

ELENA. Whichever impotent middle-aged man came up with that line deserves to be hung in the town square, <u>castrated</u>, and SHOT!

As HENRY *enters on 'hung'.*

He is dripping wet, full of exuberant energy. He recites 'The Palace of Art' by Tennyson like a Romantic poet.

HENRY. 'I built my soul a lordly pleasure-house, Wherein at ease for aye to dwell. I said, 'O Soul, make merry and carouse, Dear soul, for all is well.'

ELENA. God, not bloody Tennyson –

HENRY *dramatically dips* ELENA *back.*

Have you gone totally fucking mad?

HENRY. Mad as a stick, darling!

ELENA. Why are you sopping wet?

HENRY. I took a ritualistic dip in the sea after my press conference at the chapel. Tonight is the night that we unveil, we reveal, we subject ourselves to the merciless gaze of others!

(*Noticing the table.*) What's all this?

ELENA. I told you we're inviting a few guests for dinner after the party –

HENRY. You know I can't stand all this pomp and bloody circumstance!

KAIA. Well, it's also the Fourth of July.

HENRY. Are we considering that a holiday now?

He picks up a card and waves it.

Surely you're joking! Who invited *him*?

ELENA. You invited Ragnar, remember? He's *your* former apprentice and protégé, not mine.

HENRY. Protégé, *please*. He's in active competition with me for the Holocaust Memorial in Barcelona *and* the War Museum in Hamburg – he is aggressively trying to usurp my position!

ELENA. He doesn't need or want your position, Henry, his firm has taken off on its own.

As HENRY *towels himself off...*

HENRY. Taken off with *my* help, *my* endorsement. And styled himself as this hipster Iron Man who throws a ski slope atop a power plant and everyone proclaims he's some 'eco-conscious maverick' when really he's a media-whoring self-promoting punk!

ELENA. Do you know how you sound right now?

He throws his towel down and saunters towards her.

HENRY. Irascible, envious… irresistibly *attractive*.

ELENA. More and more by the minute.

HENRY. What do you think, Kaia? How does that *enfant terrible* stack up against me?

ELENA. Henry, don't get her involved –

HENRY. Why not let Kaia assert a voice of her own?

They look expectantly at KAIA.

KAIA. I mean, he doesn't have your *incomparable* legacy as: 'The Master of Memory and Meaning'.

HENRY. Ah ha! You hear that?

KAIA. And it's a glaring red flag when any man loves *The Fountainhead*.

HENRY. See, Kaia knows how to discern the difference between an *influencer* architect and one who has rightly earned his Stirling Prize stripes.

ELENA. It's not The Pritzker, darling.

HENRY *plants a kiss on her lips.*

HENRY. Thank you so much for that reminder, *darling*.

HENRY *picks up another card.*

And who's this? Mathilde...?

ELENA. I let Kaia invite a girlfriend to the party.

KAIA. Yes, she's a brilliant journalist who often writes about architecture –

HENRY. The *horror*.

KAIA. And is hoping to do a piece on your memorial.

HENRY. Well you know what they say...

You're either seated at the table, or listed on the menu.

KAIA *laughs, as her phone rings.*

KAIA. I should probably get this –

(*Answering.*) Hello? Hello?

ELENA. The service is shit in here – you'd think in the land of hedge-fund robber barons you'd be able to get one bloody bar.

KAIA *runs off on the phone.*

Beat. HENRY *and* ELENA *are left alone. A subtle tension surfaces between them.*

HENRY. Oh hello.

ELENA. Hello.

HENRY. I've barely seen you all day. All week in fact...

ELENA. You know I've been in back to back board meetings this week –

HENRY. I wouldn't know. I'm practically in *exile* in my own backyard.

ELENA. You made a *choice* not to sleep in the downstairs guest room.

HENRY. A choice! There's something wrong with being a guest in my own house, in my own <u>home</u>.

ELENA. So you prefer sleeping in the moldy pool house instead?

HENRY. Oh sure, playing the role of 'pool boy' is so much more appealing. At least I can harbor secret social-climbing aspirations.

ELENA. Such as?

HENRY. Oh you know, shagging a bored trophy wife or two. The ones who laze by the pool, pretending to read *Swann's Way* –

ELENA. No one reads Proust by a pool.

HENRY. Don't they?

ELENA. No one actually *reads* Proust.

Beat. HENRY *is struck with a pang of grief.*

HENRY. And you very well know the *reason* I can't stay in that bedroom, Elena.

ELENA. Please, let's not talk about it now.

HENRY. It still contains his absence, which in the dead of night feels more like a presence. He inhabits the walls, he lives in the cracks in the floor and…

Beat.

<u>I will not and cannot stay in there.</u>

ELENA *turns away, struck by her own grief.*

ELENA. Why do you think I changed it into a guest room.

HENRY. Right, you threw some paint over his imprint as if he could suddenly be *erased*!

ELENA. *Suddenly*? What were we supposed to do? Turn it into a shrine? We hadn't touched it for over ten years –

HENRY. Don't you think I know that? Why else would I be marking the anniversary tonight with my memorial –

ELENA. *Your* memorial –

HENRY. You know what I mean.

ELENA. I don't know. Is it for him, or for your adoring fans?

HENRY (*hurt*). It's for us. To preserve our son's memory.

Beat.

And I wasn't the one who insisted we'd throw some *obscene* party tonight.

ELENA. What would you have preferred? Stare at the chapel in silence while we listen to the walls of our lives caving in?

HENRY. Well when you put it that way, I guess a party does sound more fucking festive!

HENRY *tries to pull her into an embrace.*

Elena, please…

ELENA. Henry, *stop that* –

She resists him.

What do you want me to say?

HENRY. Say come back to our bedroom, come back to our *bed*…

ELENA. It's not that simple.

HENRY. Of course it is.

A moment of nearly coming together.

ELENA. I can't, we have guests coming at any minute –

HENRY. Talk to me. What do you want?

ELENA. As if you've ever been interested in *talking* –

HENRY. When have I ever not been?

ELENA *wavers, then takes a breath.*

ELENA. What I want, Henry…

HENRY. What?

Beat.

ELENA. What I want is –

RAGNAR (*offstage*). Hello hello??? Anybody home?

ELENA. Oh shit. WE'RE IN HERE!

ELENA quickly fixes herself.

HENRY (*mocking her*). 'We're in here!'

RAGNAR, British-African, a confident rising architect, enters carrying a duffle bag and a bouquet of flowers.

ELENA. The man, the myth, the Ragnar!

RAGNAR. At your service, m'lady.

He kisses ELENA.

And for you, hostess extraordinaire.

He hands her a gorgeous bouquet. HENRY *rolls his eyes.*

ELENA. Oh Ragnar, don't make me sound so *domesticated*. How did you know dahlias are my favorite?

RAGNAR. I had a very strong hunch.

ELENA. So *thoughtful* of you…

HENRY. Yes, incredibly thoughtful – to think of <u>my wife</u>!

RAGNAR. There he is: Master Builder Daddy! OG MB in the HOUSE!

RAGNAR does a little dance, then pulls HENRY *into a big hug.*

HENRY. So glad you could make it tonight, old chap.

RAGNAR. Wouldn't miss it for the world, old boss.

ELENA. And so tremendous of you to come all this way. How was your trip out here? Was traffic a total nightmare?

RAGNAR. Considering I've been to Nigeria and Norway in the past week, it wasn't too terrible.

ELENA. Why we drag ourselves out east every weekend, I don't know.

As ELENA *arranges the dahlias,* RAGNAR *wanders around, surveying their home.*

RAGNAR. But it is beautiful – this *light*.

HENRY. Yes yes, the famous light. If only the mass exodus out here every Friday wasn't worse than when the British pulled out of India.

RAGNAR. What was that like, I wonder? To have been alive during the end of such oppressive colonial rule?

HENRY. Very funny. You sure you're an architect?

RAGNAR. Learned from the best! And anyway, I took a chopper here.

ELENA. Brilliant! Unfortunately, Henry can't take them...

(*Loudly whispers.*) ... *because it triggers his flicker vertigo.*

HENRY. Which oddly doesn't affect my *hearing*.

HENRY *shoots a look at* ELENA.

RAGNAR. And what a fantastic place you've got here!

ELENA. It was a total stroke of luck. We could never afford it now.

HENRY. God, no. I apprenticed for this reclusive architect back in the nineties, when I was a penniless student, who let us stay in this decrepit little barn on the edge of his land –

ELENA. The summer I *regretfully* left London to follow Henry to New York / thinking we'd soon return –

HENRY. She means *passionately*! He became a real mentor to me, and offered to give us this old 1902 house when he died, if I promised to donate the adjacent land to a conservancy –

ELENA. And then he did die – *swimming*!

KAIA *re-enters, and sees* RAGNAR.

RAGNAR. Are you sure you didn't drown him for the real estate?

ELENA. I'll never kill and tell...

KAIA. Le Corbusier also died swimming, but off the Riviera.

RAGNAR. If there's any ideal way to go – oh, hello there!

RAGNAR *turns, surprised to see* KAIA.

HENRY. Actually, he committed *suicide*.

ELENA. Ragnar, have you met Kaia? She works for me, as my loyal editorial assistant.

RAGNAR. Yes, of course, we've met before.

> RAGNAR *and* KAIA *approach. They engage in an awkward partial handshake and cheek kiss.*

ELENA. Remind me, when was that...?

KAIA. At that book party you hosted in the city, this past winter –

RAGNAR. Gosh was it that long ago?

KAIA. Yes, almost *seven months* since we met...

HENRY. Where was I that night?

ELENA. Probably stuck in bloody Warsaw on that *dreary* restoration –

HENRY. Dreary? The Polish Royal Opera?!

ELENA. Oh Ragnar, you were just somewhere *exotic*.

RAGNAR. Norway! I got off a plane, and came straight here.

ELENA. How do you manage to look so... *fresh*.

> ELENA *squeezes* RAGNAR*'s cheek.*

RAGNAR. I did spend a few days recharging on this off-grid island, surrounded by nothing but water and wilderness... designing a blueprint for the future.

ELENA. Oh really, do tell us more...

> ELENA *and* KAIA *turn their focus to* RAGNAR.

RAGNAR. Just imagine: a carbon-neutral, self-sufficient utopian retreat, made of ancient materials like seaweed and hempcrete and thatch...

ELENA. Thatch... *wow*.   HENRY. Christ...

RAGNAR. All embodying my philosophy of 'hedonistic sustainability'.

ELENA (*to* HENRY). Hedonism? Now that's a philosophy I can get behind…

RAGNAR. Oh yeah baby! Reducing our ecological impact shouldn't come with aesthetic compromise, but should enhance our *pleasure*.

ELENA. Yes, please…

HENRY. Which you *ripped* right off Tschumi!

RAGNAR. I mean yeah, for sure it's in *dialogue* with his insane BDSM theory 'Ropes and Rules', which I learned in *your* seminar –

ELENA. Are we still talking about architecture…?

RAGNAR. And I quote: 'The game of architecture is an intricate play that has the erotic significance of *bondage*: the more numerous the restraints, the greater the pleasure.'

ELENA. Can't teach that in school anymore.

RAGNAR. No sir! Oh and I forgot to mention the best part – my design vision, plus the private island, is going up on the auction block at Christie's next week.

ELENA. Well done!

HENRY *can't take any more of this*.

HENRY. Selling off your *idea* to some tech-bro billionaire is precisely the issue with young architects today! It should be a socially conscious *process*, not a luxury asset.

Beat.

KAIA. Is it too early for a drink?

ELENA. Brilliant idea!

RAGNAR. Never too early for alcohol.

HENRY. Why don't I bring up some wines from the cellar.

ELENA. By all means. And Kaia, would you put Ragnar's bag in his room please?

HENRY. He's staying over??

ELENA. Of course – Ragnar came all the way here for *your* unveiling.

RAGNAR. I can check into a hotel, if you'd prefer –

ELENA. Don't be ridiculous!

As KAIA struggles to lift the heavy duffle bag…

RAGNAR. Please, allow me –

ELENA. No, no, let the capable young *girl*.

KAIA. To the downstairs guest room, or – ?

HENRY. <u>Absolutely not.</u>

A loaded beat.

HENRY *and* ELENA *meet eyes.*

ELENA. Put him upstairs – next to *my* master bedroom.

With a glance at RAGNAR, KAIA lugs off the duffle bag.

And Henry, the wine?

HENRY. Right.

HENRY *exits.*

Now alone, ELENA *hones in on* RAGNAR.

ELENA. Can I offer you anything to start? Martini, whiskey, tea?

RAGNAR. All of the above, please.

As she goes to get drinks…

ELENA. You're a man of multiple thirsts, aren't you, Ragnar…

RAGNAR. Oh depending on my level of *anguish*.

Beat.

I didn't know Henry had been dealing with vertigo…?

ELENA. It's been a total nightmare… an extreme case too, like he was having a seizure.

RAGNAR. Poor old boy.

ELENA. Trust me, there wasn't enough Xanax in the world to get me through that period!

Beat, diverting.

Try this, the *filthiest* olives.

She pops an olive into his mouth. He coughs, nearly choking.

RAGNAR. That'll do it.

ELENA. So… how do you *quench* such anguish when it does arise?

RAGNAR. Well, I hang out with my little monsters, my two kids.

ELENA. Right, *those*. Where is their mother?

RAGNAR. She's back in Stockholm, modeling. Or rather, 'influencing'.

ELENA. A Swede, of course. You must have a woman in every port…

RAGNAR. I rarely have the time, or interest. Or maybe they have no interest in me…

ELENA. Surely I can think of a few interested parties…

RAGNAR (*toying*). Oh really? Name one…

As ELENA *leans towards him… her phone rings.*

ELENA (*checking it*). Oh god, that *abominable* art collector.

(*Answering.*) Darling! What? Oh no, stuck on the LIE? Hang on –

ELENA *runs off to take the call as* KAIA *re-enters.*

When the coast is clear… RAGNAR *pulls* KAIA *onto his lap, kissing her neck.*

KAIA. We can't do this here – !!!

RAGNAR. Yes we can –

KAIA. No, she'll *fire* me, then *murder* me!

RAGNAR. Oh stop it –

KAIA. Yes because she's in love with you, *obsessed* with you –

RAGNAR. Don't be ridiculous –

KAIA. And you shamelessly feed into her delusional fantasy!

RAGNAR. You're my delusional fantasy –

Finally, they kiss.

ELENA (*offstage*). Right, well keep us posted. Cheers!

They hear ELENA *returning, and quickly pull far apart.*

Apparently traffic is so brutal that even New Yorkers are wishing they were in LA.

The doorbell rings.

KAIA. That must be Mathilde…

ELENA. Well, go on – *get it*.

KAIA *runs towards the front door.*

MATHILDE, *American, enters. She is luminous, a force field of energy radiating around her.*

KAIA. Thank god you're here.

HILDE. I barely made it alive from the city.

KAIA *and* HILDE *hug. They are old friends who care deeply about each other.*

Has she unleashed her reign of terror yet?

KAIA. She's just warming up, sharpening her guillotine.

ELENA (*calling out*). Girls! Where are you? GIRLS?

They flinch. KAIA *takes* HILDE*'s hand, leading her into the house.*

HILDE. Why does it feel like I'm about to breach a minefield…

KAIA. What's the worst that can happen.

HILDE. One fatal misstep?

ELENA *warmly bounds over to them.*

ELENA. There you are. Welcome, welcome! I'm Elena.

HILDE. Mathilde. Thank you so much for having me tonight.

ELENA. We love hosting all sorts of writers – consider this a 'safe space', as they say. Well, except for that one time Lou Reed came over, and said I looked like Robert Plant... but no matter now because he's *dead*!

RAGNAR. Well, well, if it isn't the notorious Mathilde.

HILDE. Ragnar, I presume.

RAGNAR *and* HILDE *cheek-kiss.*

ELENA. Don't tell me you two *know* each other.

RAGNAR. Worse! Mathilde here wrote a *savage* piece in *The Times* –

HILDE. Savage!

RAGNAR. – that called me out, *personally*, for proposing a – what did you call it? oh yes – a '*cock block* of a skyscraper'!

HILDE. I was merely commenting on those ugly new pencil towers competing to *phallically* dominate the skyline –

KAIA. Isn't that most buildings though?

ELENA. One could argue that's most <u>men</u>.

HENRY *returns, carrying a box filled with bottles of wine.*

HENRY. I found this glorious bottle of champagne that was gifted to me by Rem Koolhaas, that old bounder –

ELENA. Hen, one of our guests has arrived.

HENRY. Oh really, who's that?

As HENRY *places the box down, he freezes. He stares at* HILDE, *shell-shocked, as if he's seen a ghost.*

ELENA. This is Kaia's girlfriend, Mathilde.

HILDE. Hello...

A loaded beat of silence.

HENRY. *Mathilde…* did you say?

ELENA. Good god, Henry, are you having a *stroke*?

HENRY. I'm sorry, I could have sworn… you look…

HILDE. Everyone used to call me Hilde, but I go by Mathilde now.

HENRY redirects his focus to the champagne, but he is rattled to his core.

ELENA. So how do you girls know each other again?

KAIA. We went to Barnard together.

RAGNAR. When was that, like last year?

KAIA. You wish, Ragnar.

RAGNAR. Oh no, the Seven Sisters have stormed Southampton! Barricade your doors!

ELENA. And your *husbands*!

POP. HENRY uncorks the bottle, and pours glasses for all.

HENRY *(to* HILDE*)*. So you're a journalist, is that correct…?

HILDE. For better or worse.

KAIA. She's being humble – she's frequently published in *The Times*, and just finished her first novel.

ELENA. How enviously ambitious, for such a *tender* age.

HENRY hands a glass to RAGNAR, who takes a sip.

HENRY. How is it?

RAGNAR. God bless old Remy!

HENRY. What's your novel called?

Beat. HENRY *hands a glass to* HILDE, *meeting her gaze.*

HILDE. *Master.*

RAGNAR. Oh boy! Now that I'd like to get my hands on…

KAIA. I've read it, and I can say it's *masterful*.

RAGNAR. Seems to be 'on theme' for today. Shall we test out Tschumi's bondage theory on Kaia?

RAGNAR *clasps* KAIA's *wrists together.*

KAIA. Oh my god, Ragnar – !

KAIA *shoves him off.* ELENA *diverts the attention back to* HILDE.

ELENA. Isn't she so beautiful… for a *writer*.

RAGNAR. Are you allowed to say that?

ELENA. Why not? Are you going to *cancel* me, Ragnar.

HENRY. We should all be able to cancel our wives, on occasion.

RAGNAR. Finally a movement I could get behind!

The men jovially clink glasses.

ELENA. Terrible to admit, but historically male writers have been so much more attractive. Have you ever seen a photo of Kafka?

RAGNAR. Franz, that filthy rascal?

ELENA. I'd *fuck* Kafka. I'd let him lower his *thorax* onto my body.

HENRY. Go right ahead, darling. You might transform into a monstrous insect and never go back!

RAGNAR (*to* HILDE). So what *savage* piece on architecture are you working on now? Who's your next… *victim*?

HILDE. I'm here on assignment, actually, writing about the recent demolition of modernist landmarks out east.

HENRY. I could bang on about that subject – it's an absolute crime.

HILDE. Yes there seems to be a fetish for destroying historic homes –

RAGNAR. Did someone say *fetish*?

HILDE. I meant, like the teardown of Philip Johnson's Farney House.

RAGNAR. But speaking of! Johnson, that old queen had a *sick* Nazi fetish –

HENRY. Yeah, that's true. When I tried to teach him to my students this year, they staged a protest! Wanted to wipe his name off buildings at MoMA and Harvard –

ELENA. God, this generation is so *exhausting*, isn't it.

HILDE. But in this case, they do have a point...?

ELENA. Yes fine, *fascism aside* – if we punish past behavior based on newly imposed social codes, there will be no names on buildings left.

KAIA. I'm sorry, but architects have notoriously been some of the worst *art monsters* –

ELENA. Oh no no no, not this / *again* –

RAGNAR. But given us some of the spiciest scandals! Stanford White, come on, gotta hand it to the old panty-dropper –

KAIA. He was a total *predator*! And rightly shot by the husband of his *underage* lover!

RAGNAR (*to* HENRY). And don't we have our very own scandal to thank for your newly appointed position at Columbia...?

Beat.

HENRY (*nervous*). Pardon?

RAGNAR. After the 'untouchable' Timothy was explosively brought down – those allegations, consensual but... *crikey*.

HENRY. Oh right. Yes, it's been a nightmare inside the department...

RAGNAR. And outside! I can't believe every institution cut ties with him – the Slavery Museum, for god's sake.

ELENA. I *beg* of you, we're not drunk enough for tragic downfalls yet.

RAGNAR. No, just untragic ones!

Beat.

ELENA. Well! Now that we've gotten that insufferable debate out of the way… who wants to go for a dip before the party?

RAGNAR. Oh, you bet. *When I dip, you dip, we dip!* But Kaia must come –

KAIA. No no that's really okay –

RAGNAR. It's non-negotiable! And Henry?

ELENA. Nope, he already dipped –   HENRY. I dipped –

RAGNAR. What about you, Hilde? Oh come on, I know you want to…

HILDE. I didn't bring a swimsuit.

ELENA (*goading*). I would say you could borrow one of mine but… Why don't you just skinny dip? Surely no one here would mind.

Beat. HILDE *looks mildly horrified.*

KAIA. Elena!

ELENA. I'm *kidding*! God, you girls are such *puritans*.

HILDE. It's okay, I don't even like swimming.

ELENA. Your loss. Shall the fun ones throw on our swimming costumes and meet back here?

RAGNAR. Copy that, O Captain! My Captain!

KAIA *exchanges a glance with* HILDE *as she exits.* ELENA *takes* RAGNAR *in the other direction.*

HILDE *and* HENRY *are left alone. They stare at each other with nervous, charged energy.*

HILDE. So, you really don't remember me?

HENRY. How could I ever forget you, Hilde.

ACT ONE, SCENE TWO   31

HILDE. For a moment, it seemed like you might have.

HENRY. I was convinced I had finally lost my mind. That you were a ghost, an apparition resurrected from the past.

HILDE. But isn't that what I am…

HENRY. You've haunted me, that's for certain.

HILDE. Your dreams or your reality.

HENRY. It's often impossible to discern one from the other.

HILDE *takes a step towards him.*

HILDE. Do I look the same?

HENRY. Yes. No. You look more…

HILDE. What…

HENRY *studies her.*

HENRY. Self-possessed. Confident. Mature, I suppose…

HILDE. Are you saying I look *older*, Henry.

HENRY. Ha. No, hardly by a day.

Beat.

Though I do remember the way you used to hide your inexperience as if it were a chink in your armour, a guarded secret to nearly everyone around you.

HILDE. Everyone but you.

HENRY. Well, yes.

HILDE *moves closer to him.*

HILDE. Do you remember how long ago it was? The last time we saw each other…

HENRY. Surely a lifetime or two ago. Back when I had all my hair.

HILDE. You still have plenty, as far as I can tell.

HENRY (*insecure*). Do you think so?

HILDE *runs her hand through his hair, disarming him.*

HILDE. More than enough.

They gaze at each other. Then, she removes her hand.

It was after my junior year. The summer I was your research assistant…

HENRY *takes her glass and goes to pour her a new drink.*

HENRY. On my last book, that's right.

HILDE. *The Transgression of Architecture.*

HENRY. Now nearly out of print!

HILDE. What did you expect? Your objective was 'to arouse a discourse on the sensuality of architecture'.

HENRY. Well, I was much more idealistic back then.

HILDE. That's one way to put it.

HENRY. Dogmatic?

HILDE. *Domineering.*

HENRY. Not to you, I wasn't.

HILDE. In a different way, you were…

Beat. HENRY *hands her a refilled glass.*

HENRY. Gosh, it's all coming back to me now… those cold dark evenings after class in my office, drinking tea, or walking along the river, talking endlessly about, I don't know, abstract ideas… deconstructivism and Bachelard's *The Poetics of Space.* And your own poetry!

HILDE. Oh god, that's right…

HENRY. I remember you were so afraid to write anything real about your life… about the men you liked, or the wounds you carried.

HILDE. Still, I shared it with you.

HENRY. Yes.

Beat.

HILDE. And we talked about your loss.

HENRY. Yes, we talked a lot about that.

HILDE. And about love.

HENRY. Yes, that too…

Beat. They look at each other, a shared moment of pain passing between them.

HILDE. Remember the night we watched *Hiroshima Mon Amour* in the middle of that crazy blizzard? Trapped in your office…

HENRY. That's right! Still one of my favorite films.

HILDE. About an ill-fated love affair with a married architect. I should've know then…

HENRY. And you cried at the end, into my red scarf.

HILDE. It was so wet that you gave it to me.

HENRY. And then you wore it all semester. To *taunt* me –

HILDE. To *tempt* you…

Beat.

But you're forgetting that you cried, too.

HENRY. Yes. Because I felt your sorrow inside of me, Hilde.

She looks away, disquieted.

HILDE. No one calls me that any more.

HENRY. I'm sorry. *Mathilde* will take some getting used to.

HILDE. You know I changed it after that summer.

HENRY. Did you?

HILDE. As if I was forced to assume a new identity, and erase some tarnished version of myself…

HENRY. I hope she's not erased completely.

Beat.

HILDE. Do you remember what you used to call me…?

HENRY. My gonk! My little troll!

HILDE *laughs*.

All wild hair and strange magic.

HILDE. You used to say that I brought you good luck.

HENRY. You did! Always. Before every proposal, every competition... whenever I needed it most, you were there.

Beat.

HILDE. It was <u>ten years ago</u>. The last time we saw each other.

HENRY. No. Can that possibly be true?

HILDE. I was twenty years old.

HENRY. Was it really the same year that I lost my...?

Beat, grappling.

My god. How could it all have happened at once? All that grief and all that rapture?

HILDE. I don't know.

HENRY. You were like... this brilliant beam of light in the dark tunnel of my life that year.

HENRY *looks at her, unmoored.*

HILDE. Do you remember what you made me promise you?

HENRY. No...

HILDE. That I'd come back to you. In ten years.

HENRY. Did I...?

HILDE *looks at him, hurt and surprised he doesn't remember.*

HILDE. You never looked me up in all this time?

HENRY. Occasionally, of course, but part of me didn't want to know.

HILDE. You weren't curious about me?

ACT ONE, SCENE TWO 35

HENRY. Maybe it was too painful to imagine where you were, or who you were with... Or maybe I wanted to protect the memory of you as you were before –

He stops himself.

Before it all changed.

HILDE. Before the party, you mean.

HENRY. Well, yes.

Beat. They lock eyes.

HILDE. Do you ever think about that night...?

HENRY. Not in a very long time.

HILDE. No? You never think about me in your bedroom?

HENRY. Sometimes...

HILDE. How you bent me over your desk...

HENRY. Yes.

HILDE. And kissed me.

Beat. A memory reignited between them.

HENRY. Is that really why you came back? My promise to you?

HILDE. No, Henry... I'm not *crazy*.

HENRY. Then why?

HILDE. I was invited by Kaia, for my piece.

HENRY. Right. That's what I thought.

Beat. HENRY *exhales, relieved.*

HILDE. But I was also invited by your wife.

He stops, completely taken aback.

ELENA *and* KAIA *return, changed into swimwear.*

ELENA. Alright, let's get on with it!

KAIA. Elena, just so you're aware of time, the party starts at six p.m.

ELENA. There's plenty of time. Mathilde, you can put your stuff in the <u>downstairs</u> guest room.

ELENA glances at HENRY, expecting him to protest. But he doesn't.

HILDE. Oh, no, I'm not staying the night –

ELENA. Nonsense! It will be too late to go back to the city.

HILDE. I can just take a late Jitney back –

ELENA. <u>You're not going anywhere.</u> Kaia, show her the guest room so she can get settled in?

KAIA and HILDE head off together.

HENRY turns to confront ELENA.

HENRY. What kind of twisted game are you playing here?

ELENA. Pardon?

HENRY. You *invited* her here? Are you out of your fucking mind?

ELENA. Honestly, I don't know what you're talking about.

HENRY. Don't bullshit me, Elena. You know exactly who she is. You know *exactly* what you're doing.

ELENA. Well, maybe it's time we both reckon with the past, instead of constructing a memorial around it.

HENRY. <u>It was ten fucking years ago!</u>

ELENA. I'm painfully aware. As are you, of course. The unveiling tonight marks the anniversary of that year – <u>all of it</u>.

Beat.

HENRY. You still haven't forgiven me, is that what this is about?

ELENA. For which part, exactly?

HENRY. You want me to flagellate myself, reprise my guilt? Make a spectacle out of it for your viewing pleasure?

ELENA. I wonder what that would look like.

HENRY. You know full well we were separated when she – we had *mutually* decided to take a break at the time.

ELENA (*reeling*). We agreed to take some space because we were *bereft*, because I couldn't *look* at you without seeing Max's face, because I needed to get beyond my own resentment / of your –

HENRY. Yes I know that –

ELENA. Not so you could go off and <u>fuck your student</u>.

HENRY. I <u>never</u> fucked her, and you know that!

ELENA. But you might as well have.

Beat.

HENRY. Why are you doing this now? Why tonight of all nights?

ELENA. Can you think of a better time?

HENRY. You want me to retaliate, remind you that you had dalliances for years afterwards, that my minor infraction – <u>my one single infraction</u>! – gave you the license, the liberty, to do whatever you fucking pleased.

ELENA. We were already broken by then. The foundation had cracked clean like a bone.

HENRY. No, no, *do not* rewrite history. We had got back together – we had made a *choice* to recommit to each other, to stick it through. And we did!

ELENA. And now I'm starting to wonder why we ever bothered.

HENRY. How can you say that?

ELENA. We both know that's the truth.

Beat.

HENRY. Fine, if that's how you want to play it. Shall I call up your *friend* the district attorney, and invite him tonight too?

ELENA. Go right ahead! I'm sure he'd be delighted.

HENRY. And what about that other one, that fashion editor, and invite *her* here as well?

ELENA. For the record, both of those were entirely different.

HENRY. How?

ELENA. Because there wasn't an egregious <u>imbalance of power</u>.

Beat. HENRY *is stunned.*

HENRY. Oh. So you're *threatening* me now, is that what it's come to…?

ELENA. The <u>landscape has changed</u>, as they say.

HENRY. What is that supposed to mean?

ELENA. I guess we'll have to find out.

As the weight of this descends…

RAGNAR *enters, in tight European swim briefs.*

RAGNAR. Who is ready for the dip!

HENRY. *Oh bloody fucking christ.*

ELENA. It looks like you were born ready.

RAGNAR. Oh I was. There's Viking in my blood!

HENRY. Doesn't that qualify you to rape and pillage, not frolic in your underwear!

RAGNAR. Am I frolicking? Is this what you'd call a *frolic*?

KAIA *returns.*

ELENA. Where is Mathilde?

KAIA. I think she's still getting settled in.

ELENA. Shall we get this over with already? Henry, perhaps Mathilde can get her interview in while we are all gone.

ELENA, KAIA *and* RAGNAR *head off.*

ACT ONE, SCENE TWO 39

HENRY *paces alone, unnerved. He refills his glass of wine, and turns on music. The song 'Who Knows Where the Time Goes?' by Fairport Convention comes onto the sound system. He listens, trying to recompose himself.*

Then he begins to practice his speech...

HENRY. Good evening, welcome. Thank you for skipping your dumb American barbecues to commemorate this momentous unveiling.

HILDE *quietly re-enters.*

It has always been my dream to rebuild this church for the community, to carve it into a space amongst the sea and stars, for meditation and music... for music and meditation... and... *oh fuck me.*

HILDE *laughs.* HENRY *turns around, embarrassed.*

HILDE. Well, don't stop on my behalf...

HENRY. Oh gosh, I didn't know you were listening.

HILDE. I was having this intense flashback of your speech ten years ago – the night of the party, at the opening of your gallery downtown. Packed with your rabid fans, women and men, fawning all over you like you were a rock star...

HENRY. I never cared about that. I saw you, only you, standing in the front, distracting me with your...

HILDE. Studious presence?

HENRY. You stole the words out of my mouth.

HILDE *moves closer to him.*

HILDE. I still can't believe you climbed that wall... like a madman, a total maniac!

HENRY (*laughs*). I can't either frankly. Though I was in much better shape back then.

HILDE. Oh I bet you still could...

HENRY. Do you think?

HILDE. I remember watching you, standing at the top, cameras flashing, and thinking... did he climb up there for me?

HENRY (*earnest*). I did – only for you. I wanted to look down and know, even in my darkest hour, that I had something grounding me on this earth... someone worth coming back down for.

She takes this in, touched. Then:

HILDE. Would you do it again for me?

HENRY. I would.

HILDE. <u>Tonight?</u>

HENRY. Don't push your luck, kid.

HILDE *smiles, enjoying the hold she still has over him.*

HILDE. I never knew why you invited me that night, so *publicly...*

HENRY. There was no one like you, Hilde.

HILDE. But doesn't every man in power have his favorite? His *marked* girl – who's not singular for her brilliance, but for the way she's willing to engage in some unspoken fantasy between them.

HENRY. I never saw it as a fantasy between us.

HILDE. What did you see it as?

HENRY. It felt real, at the time. You don't think so?

Beat.

HILDE. You know, I saw you a few years ago, but you didn't see me.

HENRY. Really? Where?

HILDE. The Venice Biennale. You were giving a talk on your new Pavillon, that Vatican commission...

HENRY. Why didn't you come say hello to me afterwards?

HILDE. I was there with... someone else.

ACT ONE, SCENE TWO   41

HENRY. Oh, I see. And you didn't want him to know about me?

HILDE. Don't flatter yourself, Henry.

HENRY *smiles. He gets up to pour them drinks.*

HENRY. So what happened to him? This bloke of yours...

HILDE. Well, he was older, around *your* age. And very prominent in the art world. You'd probably know him, actually...

HENRY. Really? Who is he??

HILDE. Why, are you jealous?

HENRY. If you give me his name, I'll tell you if I am.

HILDE *flashes him a look as he approaches her again.*

HILDE. But he was divorced with kids, so our 'timing didn't align'.

HENRY. But isn't that the risk you incur by being with someone significantly older than you?

HILDE (*with conviction*). The risk isn't the age gap. It's the concession we make as the younger woman – to bend and fold ourselves into the container of a man's life, adapting to the shape of damage that preceded us.

HENRY. Then why would you do it?

HILDE. Because once you experience how an older man sees you... it *ruins* you for all others.

HENRY. How do they see you?

HILDE. As if only they possess the key that can unlock the secret about yourself.

HENRY. Are you talking about me?

HILDE. Maybe.

HENRY. Did I ruin you.

HILDE. *Forever*.

Beat. They hold each other's gaze.

Part of the reason I didn't say hello was because I never heard from you, in all these years.

HENRY. You would have *wanted* me to reach out...?

HILDE. Are you serious?

HENRY. Hilde, you have no idea how many emails I wrote you and didn't send, how many times I wanted to call you.

HILDE. Then why didn't you?

HENRY. I guess I felt accountable for what happened to us... to *you*. I couldn't face it, the aftermath...

HILDE. It was a nightmare for me.

HENRY. I know.

HILDE. <u>No, you don't.</u>

Beat.

HENRY. I assumed you never wanted to hear from me again...

HILDE. That's *all* I wanted.

Beat.

Henry, the reason you had implored me to come back was so that we could have a second chance.

HENRY. What?

HILDE. You wrote me so many letters about it that summer. I still remember the last one: '... and if you should find yourself thinking of me in ten years, as I will be thinking of you, then come and find me, little troll, and I will climb to the greatest heights to be with you.'

HENRY. God, I... I can't believe I wrote that.

HILDE. Why not?

HENRY. Hilde, come on, I must have been *delusional*! Did I actually believe that? What did I think would happen? We'd run off together, start a new life?!

HILDE. Men do it all the time.

ACT ONE, SCENE TWO 43

HENRY. Well, then I envy them.

HILDE. Why do you think that option is no longer available to you?

HENRY. Why? I mean, *look* at me, Hilde.

HILDE. I'm looking...

Beat. She takes him in.

HENRY. How could I have *deluded* myself into believing that you'd even *want* to be with me... after all this time?

HILDE. You're no older to me now than you were back then.

HENRY. But you're still so young and so disastrously beautiful and... you could be with anyone you want. Someone younger, with no baggage, a clean slate –

HILDE. That sounds fucking boring.

HENRY *smiles sadly.*

HENRY. You'd prefer a withered old man with battle scars?

HILDE. There's nothing *withered* about you, Henry.

HENRY. Hilde, I'm not the man I once was. I no longer have the fire in me I once had.

HILDE. Then maybe you need someone to *strike... a... match.*

Beat.

Don't you think about that night...

HENRY. Of course I do, I think about it all the fucking time.

HILDE. What do you think about?

HENRY. What do *you* think about?

HILDE. All of it.

HENRY. Maybe you need to remind me...

HILDE. Should I?

HENRY. Yes.

Beat. HILDE *steps into her power.*

HILDE. We were at that after-party at your place on Riverside Drive, and it was packed, everyone drinking and smoking and sweating. It was a heatwave that night, remember? And we'd been eyeing each other all night, but you were swarmed by all these *adults*. I had never felt so old yet so young at the same time. I couldn't believe I was even *there*…

Beat.

Then it got late, and guests started to leave, but for some reason I lingered…

HILDE *comes up behind him, and touches him.*

HENRY. You did…

HILDE. You found me on the fire escape, drinking warm white wine, waiting to watch the fireworks over the park.

HENRY. You had on this little blue dress, I remember. The strap kept slipping off your shoulders…

HILDE. Yes. And I asked where you wrote in the house, and you said at this desk in your bedroom. And I said *show it to me*… I want to see it.

HILDE *leads him over to a chair, and he sits.*

HENRY. Yes…

HILDE. So you took me there, and locked the door behind us… We had never been alone together like that, outside your office… my heart was pounding like a drum in my chest. And you led me to your desk, in that alcove, and showed me some of your drawings, but I was barely listening…

Beat.

And then I leaned on the desk, like this…

She provocatively leans over the table.

And you came close to me then, and gently stroked my hair. I felt your hands trembling, you were so afraid to touch me. You said your wife hadn't touched you in a year…

HENRY (*pained*). No, not since…

ACT ONE, SCENE TWO 45

HILDE. And then I told you to kiss me…

HENRY. Yes, you did…

> HILDE *turns around. She takes his hand, sliding it over her body.*

HILDE. And you kissed my neck, my shoulders, my breasts, everywhere but my mouth, your hands sliding up my bare legs, beneath my dress. I could barely stand, I wanted you so much. And then you bent me over the desk, like this…

She leans back on the table, her hands behind her. He is sitting between her legs now.

HENRY. And then what happened…

HILDE. And you said we can't do this, but it was too late. Your mouth was between my thighs, your hand grasping mine, and I felt my whole body bursting like the fireworks outside the window.

Beat.

No man had ever done that to me before…

HENRY. I didn't know that.

> HENRY *stands up, his desire so intense it torments him.* HILDE *is still leaning back on the table so that he is standing above her now.*

HILDE. Then I got on my knees and called you Master – <u>my</u> Master Builder.

HENRY. Yes…

HILDE. And when I looked up, I saw you were weeping. Tears were streaming down your face, onto my hair…

HENRY. God, I was so ashamed.

HILDE. You were?

HENRY. I'd never known such ecstasy and agony all at once.

Beat. Then, quietly…

HILDE. But we never slept together.

HENRY. No.

HILDE. Though I dreamt about it all the time…

Beat.

HENRY. I was so in love with you, Hilde.

HILDE. Were you…?

HENRY. That night was the last time I felt *anything*. My heart has been closed since, a locked door bolted shut. No crack for light to seep through.

Beat.

So when I saw you today… it was as if a flash of lightning shot through me, at full voltage. The memory of you, the memory of desire. For so long I tried to bury it but now…

HILDE *takes his face in her hands, moved.*

HILDE. I was in love with you too.

HILDE *strokes his cheek. As they draw closer and closer –*

ELENA *and* RAGNAR *return to the house, wet from the ocean.*

HILDE *and* HENRY *abruptly pull apart.*

ELENA. You were such a little pussy!

RAGNAR. It was practically Baltic! Colder than the English Channel! I can't feel my legs!

ELENA. What happened to all that Viking in your blood?

RAGNAR. I must've left it up north somewhere.

ELENA *vigorously rubs* RAGNAR's *body. Making a show of it in front of* HENRY.

ELENA. Is that better?

RAGNAR. Much. Now all I need is a hot shower.

HENRY. And I need a cold one immediately.

ELENA. Are you going to use the pool house?

HENRY. So it seems.

HENRY *exits.* KAIA *returns, carrying wet towels.*

ELENA. Mathilde, I forgot to inquire, did you invite a date tonight?

HILDE. Oh, no… there's no date to speak of.

ELENA. Don't tell me *you're* single too.

HILDE. Alas, it's true.

ELENA. What is wrong with you two girls? Both of you, so lovely and bright, yet no one has snapped you up?

KAIA. I'm not sure that's the issue…

ELENA. See the advantage of a woman *my age* is we no longer need the charade of marriage and monogamy to validate us. But sadly, you two girls can't ignore the deafening *tick-tock tick-tock* of your biological clocks. Look at Kaia, always pining after some *pathetic* man –

KAIA. What? No / I'm not – !

ELENA. Which is why I'm setting her up tonight with that art collector.

Beat.

RAGNAR. Really? That filthy old lech?!

HILDE (*in defence*). Actually, I think Kaia already has a man in her life.

ELENA *stops, turns to* KAIA.

ELENA. Then how come I haven't heard about him?

KAIA. She's just saying that –

ELENA. You sneaky little tart. Who is he? Go on, out with it!

KAIA. It's no one special, trust me.

KAIA *and* RAGNAR *exchange an awkward glance.*

ELENA. Well, maybe the truth will come out with a little *lubrication.* Everyone take a dressing drink, and off you go! Ragnar, you can use the shower in my master bedroom… it's much *harder* pressure.

RAGNAR. Master it is.

ELENA. I'll show you upstairs.

> RAGNAR *and* ELENA *exit together.*

KAIA. I can't believe you said that!

HILDE. I know, I'm sorry! I just couldn't bear it any longer.

KAIA. Oh no. Do you think she suspects anything?

HILDE. No, don't worry. She's too consumed with her own power to recognize the subversive threat of yours.

KAIA. If only I had any. God, it's like watching her pry apart the waves of feminism with a crowbar.

Beat.

HILDE. But I don't understand… what is her objective with all of this? Why did she invite me?

KAIA. That's the thing… there's usually a method to her madness, but I can't discern what it is. She only acts unhinged when she's feeling deeply insecure…

HILDE. Insecure about her marriage?

KAIA. About herself.

> ELENA *re-enters in a silk kimono, on the phone.*

ELENA. What? No, I told you that if the flowers aren't delivered by five p.m., then I will send my assistant over to your farm even if she has to *blow* the farmer himself!

> HILDE *and* KAIA *exchange a glance, wincing.* ELENA *hangs up.*

Kaia, would you mind terribly calling the flower farm and handling this?

KAIA. Of course.

> KAIA *exits.* HILDE *makes a move to leave.*

ELENA. I'm absolutely starving! You look like you must be too.

HILDE. Maybe a little.

ELENA. Always wise to have a snack before the party so you don't bite anyone's head off.

ELENA *goes off to get some food.*

(*Calling out.*) So did you interrogate my husband yet?

HILDE (*nervous*). Excuse me?

ELENA. For your *Times* piece. Did he give you any profound quotes on modernism?

HILDE. Oh yes, something along those lines.

ELENA *returns with a packet of crackers.*

ELENA. You're a very talented writer, I must say.

HILDE. Thank you.

ELENA. But it was your fiction that blew me away – I was quite impressed.

HILDE. My fiction...?

ELENA. The manuscript of your novel, *Master*. I devoured it in one sitting, I couldn't put it down.

HILDE *is taken aback as* ELENA *shoves a cracker into her hand.*

Try this, a proper cream cracker – I stuff them in my suitcase whenever I'm back in London. I promise, a carb won't kill you yet.

HILDE (*baffled*). I'm sorry... how did you read the book??

ELENA. Mathilde, I'm the head of a major publishing empire. If I want something, I can track it down without even having to slit someone's throat.

HILDE. Though occasionally you do anyway.

ELENA. Only when I'm in need of a little thrill.

Beat. HILDE *tries to recompose herself.*

HILDE. So what did you think of it?

ELENA. Well, through a *critical* lens, I thought it was brazen, radical even, exploring the complex ambiguity of sexual agency in our current era, *blah blah blah*.

HILDE. And... through a personal lens?

ELENA. That's an entirely different question.

HILDE. Isn't it always.

ELENA. No, but I recognized the story as a rather familiar one.

HILDE (*uneasily*). How so...

ELENA. Precocious college girl seduced by eminent tyrant of an *architect*, her professor. But the twist? It's not about patriarchal abuse of power, not a neat account of victimhood. No.

Beat.

Instead, it paints an unflattering portrait of his wife – whose allegiance *problematically* lies with her husband.

HILDE. That's one way to see it.

ELENA. A highly controversial take, in this inflammatory climate.

HILDE. I'm not interested in creating politically correct art.

ELENA. And normally, I'm not interested in reading any.

Beat.

Mathilde, darling, let's cut through the pleasantries. I know who you are, and you know that I know that.

HILDE. Honestly, at first I wasn't so sure...

ELENA. But you accepted my invitation tonight. Why?

HILDE. My burning curiosity?

ELENA. You can do better.

HILDE. My penchant for self-destruction...

Beat.

ELENA. I think you'll find yourself surprised by my intentions. Since reading your book, it triggered a lot of... *self-reflection*

ACT ONE, SCENE TWO 51

on my part – a rare phenomenon, believe me. It rattled me, I suppose, to see how you interpreted the events of the past.

HILDE. To be clear, it's *fiction*, not a memoir.

ELENA. And I appreciate the distinction. But Hilde, first and foremost, I realize that I owe you a genuine apology.

HILDE. Okay...

Beat.

ELENA. I know it was a long time ago, but I would like a chance to explain my perspective. When I heard something *transpired* between you and my husband – when that nasty rumor reached me – I'm afraid that I reacted rather... *insensitively*.

HILDE. That's a mild way to put it.

ELENA. It was at a time when I was blindsided by grief after losing my son – my entire world had gone pitch-black.

HILDE. I know, and I'm sorry for that.

ELENA. So you must understand. I couldn't bear to lose my husband, in addition to my only child. I did what I had to do to preserve what I had left of my family – at all costs.

HILDE. At the expense of my own future, you mean.

ELENA. Isn't that a touch dramatic? Trust me, if you had been in my place, you would have done the same.

HILDE. I would *never* have done what you did.

ELENA. You don't know until you've experienced it.

Beat. HILDE *confronts her.*

HILDE. You made my life a living *hell*, Elena. You publicly slut-shamed me – as a student. As a woman. I was forced to drop my double major in architecture, which I had worked so hard for –

ELENA. That was your *choice* –

HILDE. And you tried to *discredit* me from going to grad school! I read the emails you sent to the Dean of Columbia and Yale – *disparaging* my character, claiming that I would be a liability. And since you were this so-called 'champion of women', this 'advocate for female empowerment', they listened to you!

ELENA. Well, you ended up going to NYU.

HILDE. After taking years off! And I had no resources, no money – it derailed *everything* I had worked for.

ELENA. It seems like you still came out on top.

HILDE. Wow.

Beat. ELENA *recalibrates.*

ELENA. Hilde, I'm sorry. I admit, I acted out of self-preservation, not empathy. And though I'm not justifying how I handled the situation, that depth of loss can drive a woman to *madness*.

HILDE. But I experienced a different kind of loss.

ELENA. Of what? A loss of *innocence*?

HILDE. I was twenty years old – I was still a virgin.

ELENA *can't mask her surprise.*

ELENA. And now I recognize how young you were… how *impressionable*. And though I'm not asking for your forgiveness, I invited you tonight as an olive branch – a chance to make it up to you in some way.

HILDE. How?

ELENA. By offering you a moment of reckoning.

Beat. HILDE *tries to leave the room.*

HILDE. I'm sorry, I don't want to talk about this anymore –

ELENA. Just hear me out –

HILDE. I should leave, I should never have come here tonight –

ELENA. Please, listen to me. Let me rectify the wrongs of the past.

HILDE. It's a little too late for that now.

ELENA. No, it's exactly the right time, exactly the right moment! A decade ago, it was a completely different world, but now we have this global movement of women, raising their voices –

HILDE. You don't even *believe* in all that!

ELENA (*earnest*). Look, I was like you once… in thrall to my older professor, a famous poet, when I was eighteen at uni back home. I had grown up poor, my father was a brute… tried to strangle my mother one night when he was piss drunk. That's what I had known.

Beat.

So then to have this celebrated writer, who looked like Ted Hughes, give *me* attention, make *me* feel special… But in the end, I was just one of so many others, taken advantage of and tossed out.

HILDE. Why are you telling me this?

ELENA. Because perhaps you're directing your anger at the wrong person.

Beat.

HILDE. I don't think so.

ELENA. Are you so sure?

HILDE (*wavering*). Yes…

ELENA. I mean, Hilde. Do you really think you've been his one and only 'little troll'?

Beat. Piercing.

You may have been naive then, but don't be any longer.

Beat. HILDE *shifts, questioning the truth.*

HILDE. What do you want?

ELENA. I heard your book hasn't sold yet.

HILDE. Not yet…

ELENA. Twenty rejections and counting?

HILDE. It's a tough market.

ELENA. So let me help you sell it.

HILDE. Why would you do that?

ELENA. I told you, I owe you an enormous debt.

HILDE. And what do *you* get out of it?

ELENA. Hilde, it's no secret who you are writing about – Henry is a very public figure. There will be questions you'll be forced to answer, whether you want to or not.

HILDE. So you're trying to control the narrative?

ELENA. No, I'm trying to help you *reclaim* your own.

HILDE. I don't understand…

ELENA. Young readers today demand authenticity – they want the truth in the trauma. If you don't reveal your own personal history, then you aren't justified to be the mouthpiece of it.

Beat.

HILDE. You're asking me to come out with my story??

ELENA. If you did, I guarantee your book will sell within a week.

HILDE. I'm sorry, *why* would you want to expose your own husband?

ELENA. Let's just say I have my reasons.

HILDE. Are you trying to redeem yourself, or seek retribution?

ELENA. Why can't a woman do both at the same time.

Beat. HILDE *weighs this intractable decision.*

HILDE. So what are you asking me to do about it *tonight*?

ELENA. I think you should confront Henry… tell him you're considering coming out with your story.

HILDE. At his *own* party?

ELENA. Wasn't it at that party, exactly ten years ago when you – when he crossed a line?

HILDE *nods*.

So be smart, Mathilde. You've been waiting for this reckoning long enough.

HENRY *returns*.

As he walks into the room, he stops before HILDE *and* ELENA. *The air crackling between them.*

Then:

HENRY. Are we ready for the party?

Blackout.

ACT TWO

Scene One

Later that evening.

The party. It's buzzing with festive flowing summer energy. Lights. Candles. Flowers. Champagne. Music.

The CHAPEL *is aglow with the golden shades of magic hour.*

KAIA *and* RAGNAR *stand beside each other with cocktails.*

RAGNAR. Your paramour is staring right at you.

KAIA. Who?

RAGNAR. The paunchy art collector.

KAIA. Stop. Is he…?

RAGNAR. Like he's undressing you with his eyes, waiting to feast on your tight, tender… *tendons.*

KAIA. You really don't take me seriously, do you.

RAGNAR. Of course I do – I take it seriously you might get *eaten.*

KAIA. No, it's all a power play to you. Just like it is to your puppet master, Elena.

RAGNAR. Oh baby, how can you say that?

KAIA. Then why don't you tell her about us.

RAGNAR. Kaia, please.

KAIA. If you're so serious, then why don't you tell her you've been seeing me for the past seven months.

RAGNAR. Oh come on, now you're acting like a little nutter!

KAIA. Why wouldn't you?

RAGNAR. Well… it just wouldn't be very *polite* of us, would it?

ACT TWO, SCENE ONE 57

KAIA. Polite? Wow. You're under her spell just like everyone else.

ELENA *makes her grand entrance in a jaw-dropping, revealing ensemble. She looks stunning.*

Speak of the devil...

ELENA. So are we having fun yet? Or do we all need to start jumping into the pool!

RAGNAR. Looks like the fun just arrived! You look ravishing, Elena.

KAIA. You really do...

ELENA. Do I? I wore this to a debauched *Eyes Wide Shut* party thrown by a German media baron – which I barely escaped intact – and needed a reason to wear it since. So I thought, why not *scandalize* an art world asshole or two.

RAGNAR. Mission accomplished.

ELENA *looks up at the* CHAPEL, *taking it in.*

ELENA. So what do we think?

RAGNAR. Sort of looks like a drunken pyramid, no?

ELENA. Is that meant to be a steeple?

RAGNAR. Sometimes a steeple is not just a steeple.

KAIA. I think it's a *masterpiece.*

ELENA. Then maybe you should do Henry's PR! Kaia, where's your friend?

KAIA. I don't know, I haven't seen her.

HENRY *enters. He climbs the exterior of the* CHAPEL, *even higher than before. He gazes down, the master of his domain. He anxiously scans the party for* HILDE, *but doesn't see her...*

The GUESTS *notice him, clink their glasses until a hush comes over the party.*

HENRY. Good evening, welcome. Thank you all for coming out tonight to mark this very special unveiling, and on this glorious fourth of July no less – what better way to celebrate your independence than at a party thrown by tyrannical Brits!

Beat. Laughter.

Before the orgiastic festivities begin, and on a more sober note... I'd like to say a few words on the chapel itself. The desire to remember – to stitch together the past and present – unites our reasons for building for both the living and the dead. As many of you know, we are standing on hallowed ground, atop the carcass of this historic landmark from 1832, the old Whaler's Church, that was destroyed in a tragic fire eleven years ago. It has always been my dream to rebuild this site for the greater community, to shape it into a sanctuary of meditation and memory. So you might find yourself asking: why on earth does it resemble a misshapen pyramid? But I can assure you, there is a reason.

Beat.

When I was imagining the church's next life, I returned to its original structure – which was built in an Egyptian Revival style. And it got me thinking of the mystery of the ancient pyramids of Giza... There is a moving theory that the pyramids were built as star shafts – in alignment with Orion's Belt, their peaks pointing due north towards the undying stars, which they called 'The Indestructibles'. So their purpose, as it were, was to serve as a stairway to heaven, a portal from life into the celestial afterlife...

HENRY *falters, struck with grief, as the setting sun directly strikes the* **CHAPEL**, *lighting it ablaze. Suddenly, he is struck with a brief, violent flash of vertigo.*

The party whispers, concerned...

But then he sees **HILDE**, *parting the crowd. A mythic vision in a shimmering dress. She smiles up at him. Her presence fills him with renewed strength.*

As the sun shifts lower, **HENRY** *regains his balance, and carries on...*

My hope is that the chapel becomes a North Star for all, an unwavering light in an often dark sky. It is both a monument

ACT TWO, SCENE ONE 59

for the future, and a memorial to the past. One that I have dedicated to the memory of my beloved son Max, who we lost, but whose indomitable spirit lives on...

Beat. Emotional.

May it be a space for music and poetry, for reflection and discovery, for the community to gather together in all seasons in celebration of art and life. Cheers, and party on!

Cheers. The party resumes.

HENRY *descends the structure, sweating and out of breath. He tries to reach* HILDE, *but he's bombarded by a barrage of* GUESTS.

Before he can extricate himself, HILDE *slinks out of sight.*

HENRY *spots* KAIA *standing alone.*

Am I getting older, or is my tolerance for these sorts of things getting lower?

KAIA. Or is everyone here intolerable to begin with.

HENRY. Unlike you to sound as curmudgeonly as I am.

KAIA. Maybe I've absorbed it, like second-hand smoke.

HENRY. What's the matter? You look much too morose to be celebrating...

KAIA. I'm feeling festive on the inside, can't you tell?

They both watch ELENA *flirting with* RAGNAR.

HENRY. Where's your girlfriend? Did she abandon you?

KAIA. Apparently. I don't know where she escaped to...

HENRY. Leaving you alone to fend for yourself? What a turncoat.

KAIA. Aren't you referring to <u>your wife</u>.

Beat.

Oh god sorry, I didn't mean that –

HENRY. No, that's perfectly alright.

KAIA. You know what? I'm not sorry. I shouldn't disclose this, but I'm three negronis deep so I'm gonna say it anyway: she's planning to file for a <u>divorce</u>.

HENRY. *What...?*

KAIA. She's hired a lawyer, started the paperwork, the whole thing. And maybe I'm the traitor for telling you, but I don't want you to be blindsided, that's all.

As HENRY *reacts, gobsmacked...*

'Sympathy for the Devil' by The Rolling Stones begins to play.

ELENA. Ooohh I LOOOOOVE this song!

Across the party, ELENA *begins to dance, uninhibited.*

KAIA. Oh dear god...

ELENA *lures* RAGNAR *into her dance.*

ELENA. Raaaaagnar, come dance with me!

RAGNAR. Oh no no you don't want me to do that –

ELENA. Oh yes I fucking do!

ELENA *and* RAGNAR *engage in a sensual, attention-grabbing dance. The* GUESTS *watch and cheer them on.*

Until HENRY *erupts and storms over to them.*

HENRY *(exploding).* What in god's name are you doing??!!

ELENA. I'm just having a bit of FUN! Remember that?

HENRY. Fun? You call making a scene at my own party... *fun?*

ELENA. *Your* party. *Your* memorial. Thank you for reminding me why the fuck I'm even here!

HENRY. This was your bloody idea to begin with!

RAGNAR *intercepts, physically holding* HENRY *back.*

RAGNAR. Hey mate, relax, let's all take a beat –

HENRY. Don't fucking touch me!

ACT TWO, SCENE ONE 61

HENRY *pushes him off with such force that* RAGNAR *stumbles backwards, nearly knocking over a tray.*

ELENA. Wow, Henry, bravo! I didn't know you could still *get it up* like that!

HENRY. Have you gone fucking mental?!

ELENA. I think that's the first time you've acted like a MAN in years! In fact, I'm so *aroused* that this deserves a toast! But I need champagne – someone BRING ME MY CHAMPAGNE!

A GUEST *runs off.*

What should my toast be about? Shall I play the part of the loyal, long-suffering wife of the narcissistic architect, who deserves a prize herself for tolerating those grueling years of absence – all the nights spent at the office, all those months spent in Germany or Japan. No, that's not quite right...

HENRY. *Will you please lower your voice?!*

ELENA. Because I didn't mind that at all. It gave me time to focus on my own career, which you hardly paid attention to. No, it wasn't your absence that bothered me, but your abject indifference.

A GUEST *returns with a bottle of champagne.*

Just in time!

ELENA *grabs the bottle.*

Behind her, the CHAPEL *is aflame with the shades of sunset.*

RAGNAR. Well I guess it's all gone tits up...

ELENA *commands the attention of the party. The* GUESTS *clink their glasses.*

ELENA. I'd like to make a toast... to my dear husband. They say all architects strive to endure beyond their deaths... but how many are lucky enough to survive beyond their first wives?

She points the bottle at HENRY.

While there were many times I wanted to kill you during the agonizing duration of this project... I remain in awe of your *mastery* and passion and dedication to caring for the tragic wreckages of the past – even if that means abandoning your own. CHEERS!

ELENA *pops the bottle and champagne explodes.*

HENRY *can't bear anymore of this. He pushes through the crowd and escapes from the party.*

Scene Two

Exterior of the house. A purple dusk has settled over the dunes. The noise of the party fades into the background.

HILDE *is standing in the watery shadows.*

After a moment, HENRY *runs in, his world swirling. He stops when he sees* HILDE.

HENRY. What are you doing here?

HILDE. The same thing you're doing.

HENRY. Seeking shelter from the storm.

HENRY *stares at her, transfixed.* HILDE *glows in the moonlight.*

God you look too beautiful to be real...

HILDE. Do you say that to all the girls, Master Builder...

HENRY. There was never anyone but you, Hilde.

HILDE *comes closer, taking his hands.* HENRY *closes his eyes.*

When I was up there, giving that speech... it was so terrible. My vertigo returned for a brief moment. For years after the fire, the years after you left –

HILDE. *I never left.*

ACT TWO, SCENE TWO 63

HENRY. I'm sorry, I... I'd be on site at one of my buildings, and a flash of light could send the world spinning around me, pulling me down into a black hole. As if I might *die*. Then tonight, I felt it again...

Beat.

Until I saw you. And everything steadied then... the sea... the trees... the horizon. My own heartbeat...

He breaks down.

When I see you, Hilde, I feel so far away from the life I once imagined. I see what I had loved, and now what I have lost.

HILDE. You haven't lost me. I'm right here...

She tenderly strokes his face.

Kiss me...

HENRY. No, I can't...

HILDE. Henry...

HENRY. If I do, you'll destroy me. I'll burn into a heap of ashes.

HILDE. Then I'll risk your demolition...

Finally, they kiss.

After a moment, HENRY *tries to pull away from her, agonized –*

HENRY. Fuck, we can't do this, I can't do this –

HILDE. Yes you can.

They kiss again, more heatedly, and begin to undress each other. Then he pulls her in the direction of the dunes. As they disappear...

ELENA *emerges from the shadows. She has been watching part of this scene. Her face struck with shock and hurt and betrayal. A beam of light crosses her face, then passes into darkness.*

Scene Three

Exterior of the house. Later.

HILDE *and* HENRY *re-enter from the sea. They are in a blissful, dreamy post-coital state, pulling on their clothes.*

HILDE. We can't stay here all night!

HENRY. No no no, you're absolutely forbidden to leave –

HILDE. The party's not even over yet. They'll start to wonder –

HENRY. I don't give a fuck about anyone but you.

   HENRY *pulls her into him.* HILDE *pretends to struggle, then yields.*

HILDE. Okay okay, I surrender – !

HENRY. Good girl.

   They kiss, a deep, passionate kiss.

   Why don't we abscond together... take a trip somewhere.

HILDE. Where should we go?

HENRY. I'll whisk you away and take you on a... Scandinavian architectural adventure!

HILDE. Ooooh I've never been...

HENRY. Do you remember where I once promised to take you? The most sublimely serene place in the world... the inspiration for my own chapel.

HILDE. Oh yes... you did promise me! In Stockholm?

HENRY. Yes! Gunnar Asplund's Woodland Cemetery.

HILDE. Nothing more romantic than *death*...

HENRY. But it is! The most romantic. Just imagine... together, we would wend our way through the vast green pine forest, until we found the gravel path that leads towards the Woodland Chapel... where the deep portico continues the darkness of the woods itself. And I'd take your hand, and we'd pass beneath the bronze Angel of Death, and sit inside in the holy darkness, illuminated only by the skylight above, and there I would kiss you...

He kisses her.

And my love would be sealed in the most sacred space.

HILDE. Your *love*...?

HENRY. Yes.

HILDE. For Nordic Classicism? Or for me...

HENRY. For both of course.

HILDE turns around, leaning back into his chest. HENRY lovingly wraps his arms around her, stroking her hair and arms.

HILDE. And then... where would we go?

HENRY. Well, maybe a scenic drive along the fjords of Peer Gynt Road, through the kingdom of trolls, so you can visit your little troll friends...

He tickles her, and she laughs.

HILDE. And then...

HENRY. Then... I would take you with me back to New York.

Beat. Dreamily.

And I'd build us a new house on the ocean.

HILDE. A *house*?

HENRY. Yes. Perhaps a simple shape, white and glass, open to the blue expanse of sea and sky from all angles. The light changing at all times of day, of seasons... and no ghosts there to haunt us.

HILDE. Sounds like a dream.

HENRY *(fervid)*. But it could be real. It could be ours.

HILDE. If only...

Beat. HILDE *sits up.* HENRY *detects her hesitation.*

HENRY. Hilde... do you ever think about having a family?

HILDE. What...?

HENRY. I mean like a child of your own.

She stops, tensing.

HILDE. Not *tonight* I don't...

HENRY. No, I know, I –

A pained beat.

Sorry, I realized my son used to play out here, so... I was thinking of that.

HILDE. Oh I didn't know...

HENRY. I just want you to have everything you deserve. That's all.

Beat. HENRY *tries to backtrack.*

Yet HILDE *feels a shift within her body.*

God, how did I wait ten years to feel this way again?!

HILDE. You didn't *wait*...

HENRY. Yes I did! I waited and waited.

HILDE. You didn't even *remember* your own promise to me.

HENRY (*sincere*). I was never with anyone else, Hilde.

HILDE. Oh come on, that can't be true.

HENRY. It is true! You know I was married this entire time...

HILDE. That doesn't prove anything, especially not to your wife.

HENRY. Foolish of me to think it did. But I swear to you I'm telling the truth.

HILDE. I still don't *believe* you...

HENRY *approaches* HILDE *again.*

HENRY. You were the one who wasn't tied down.

HILDE. What's that supposed to mean...?

HENRY. Surely you were running about town, wild and free, a naughty siren troll destroying the hearts and bodies of men...

HILDE. I thought I was *your* troll...

HILDE *stands over him.*

Their power dynamic palpably turning.

HENRY. Then more like a dangerous bird of prey, maybe a red-tailed hawk...

HILDE. Is that so?

HENRY. Ravenous and rapacious, carnivorously hunting for meat.

HILDE. And what if I am...

HENRY. Are you?

HILDE *provocatively sinks down onto his chest.*

HILDE. Why shouldn't I go hunting too? Lure my prey... sink my teeth into his flesh...

She wraps her hand around his throat, gently choking him.

...and *swallow* him down whole.

HENRY. How many victims have you claimed?

HILDE. Wouldn't you like to know...

HENRY. Tell me. How many men have you had?

They lock eyes, something primal unleashed between them.

HILDE. You want a number?

HENRY. Yes. I want to know, I *need* to know. Each and every one.

HILDE. Why does it matter?

HENRY. Don't I deserve emotional retribution?

HILDE. Inflicting it or receiving it.

HENRY. Have you been with anyone older than me?

HILDE. Yes.

> HENRY *slips his hand beneath her dress.* HILDE *moans softly.*

HENRY. The man who took you to the Venice Biennale?

HILDE. Yes.

HENRY. And he was powerful?

HILDE. Very.

HENRY. Did you enjoy it?

HILDE. Fucking him?

HENRY. Yes…

HILDE. He taught me a lot…

HENRY. Like what? Tell me one thing.

HILDE. He taught me… that sometimes the most intense pleasure comes from the deepest pain.

HENRY. That doesn't sound very fun.

HILDE. But isn't it true?

> *Beat.*

> And he would ask me if he *owned* me. He would make me repeat it back to him.

> HENRY *relinquishes all control to her.*

HENRY. Say it to me.

HILDE. Now?

HENRY. Go on.

HILDE. Yes, you *own* me. Yes, I *belong* to you.

HENRY. And you liked that?

HILDE. Yes…

> *Beat.*

I liked feeling that my power over him was so intense... the only way he could assert his own was to possess me, to *dominate* me.

HENRY. But you didn't let him.

HILDE. I let him *think* he did.

Beat.

HENRY. Were you in love with him?

HILDE. No...

Beat.

Yes.

HENRY (*vulnerable*). Are you in love with me?

Beat. HILDE *stops, unsettled.*

HILDE. Henry...

HENRY. Are you?

She looks at him, unable to answer. It's no longer a game; the incursion of reality has slipped in.

Say yes. I want you to tell me that you are –

HILDE. We barely even *know* each other now...

HENRY. I've always known you, Hilde, *always*.

Beat.

Tell me that we'll be together from now on –

HILDE. Henry, you sound crazy!

HENRY. No one else, only me –

HILDE. You're still married!

HENRY. That didn't stop you before.

Beat.

I'm sorry.

In the distance, they hear the clamor of party guests.

HILDE. Someone's coming back –

HENRY (*fervently*). I want to give you the world, Hilde. Let me. I want to take you everywhere with me, and make up for all this lost time –

HILDE (*sadly*). But how can we?

HILDE looks back at him, deeply conflicted.

HENRY. I *promise* you, Hilde, you'll see.

HENRY kisses her again, and they part.

Scene Four

The atrium. (As in Act One, Scene Two.)

The table has now been beautifully set for the dinner.

ELENA *wanders in, vaping. Unhinged.*

She is startled to find RAGNAR *there – who reacts as if caught.*

RAGNAR. Oh I'm sorry –

ELENA. You scared me!

RAGNAR. That's what all the girls say.

ELENA *tries to pull herself together.*

ELENA. I didn't expect to find you here…

RAGNAR. I was… in search of the bathroom.

ELENA. Wrong door.

RAGNAR. And what are you in search of…?

ELENA. Privacy. Whiskey. *You…*

RAGNAR. Well I can help you with two out of three. Shall I go get you one?

RAGNAR *makes a deliberate move towards the door, but* ELENA *pulls him back into the room.*

ELENA. Oh no no no, we need the *special* whiskey, the decade-you-were-born whiskey, the retainer-for-a-divorce-lawyer kind of whiskey.

RAGNAR. The very best kind.

As ELENA *goes off to locate the whiskey...*

KAIA *pops up from a hiding place near the doorway.* RAGNAR *quickly gestures for her to hide again...*

ELENA *returns with a bottle, and pours two glasses.*

ELENA. Here we are.

RAGNAR. Cheers to...

ELENA. ...to treason!

RAGNAR. Happy Treason Day, Colonial Peasants!

Beat.

I saw that on a T-shirt somewhere.

They clink and drink. RAGNAR *makes another attempt to leave...*

Shall we go back out to the party?

ELENA. Noooo, I can't bear it. All those ghastly city people, plotting a hostile takeover of each other's companies or wives. You know this little man had the balls to ask me tonight if the rumor was true that I was being replaced by a thirty-year-old – and I didn't know if he meant my job or my marriage!

RAGNAR. What did you say?

ELENA. I asked if the rumor was true that his wife was fucking their kid's tennis instructor.

RAGNAR. Well done. And is she?

ELENA. No, but now he *thinks* she is.

They clink again. RAGNAR *sits down beside her at the table.*

RAGNAR. So then why do you stay out here?

ELENA. I ask myself that every summer...

Beat.

But this house... what it holds.

RAGNAR. I understand. A home can contain a library of memory, and once you leave it... it's as if all the books that hold the history of your life are lost.

ELENA. Yes. That's exactly how it feels.

Beat. ELENA *looks away, mournful.*

RAGNAR. Are you alright?

ELENA. Why? Do I not look it?

RAGNAR. No I didn't say that! I just meant... it must be an emotional night for you, with the tribute of the memorial.

ELENA. Oh... yes, I suppose it is.

Beat.

RAGNAR. You know I met your son once. He must've been four or five.

ELENA (*jarred*). Oh. Really...?

RAGNAR. It was the year Henry trusted me to lead my first team, for that library upstate – a life-changing opportunity, really, for an immigrant kid like me. And I idolized him, the way he did it all – legendary architect, professor, writer, with a gorgeous wife to boot? He was unrivaled. Not to say he didn't have his ego, his temper, his flaws –

ELENA. Believe me, he has them all...

RAGNAR. Still, he was a master of the universe. But that day, when your son came to visit the site... it was the first time I saw a different side of Henry – as a normal *dad*, warm and caring and sort of goofy. And your son was so proud to be there with him, wearing his little hard hat, carrying around this construction Lego dude... he clearly *worshipped* his father.

Beat.

And I thought: *this* is what I want one day. To build this *legacy*.

ELENA. I still have that Lego...

Beat. ELENA *smiles sadly.*

RAGNAR. Did you ever want another child?

ELENA. Oh...

RAGNAR. I'm sorry, that was inappropriate of me –

ELENA. No, no I...

Beat.

I did once, yes. Terribly. And we tried at one point. But I miscarried twice and then... by the time I was ready again, it was too late...

Beat. ELENA *wipes her eyes.*

RAGNAR. I'm so sorry –

ELENA. No it's okay – it's just, no one ever asks me that anymore.

RAGNAR. I really shouldn't have –

ELENA. No, I appreciate that you did.

ELENA *touches him. She notices a tattoo running up his inner arm.*

What does your tattoo say?

RAGNAR. '*A chaque souvenir je transportais des pierres*'...

'With each memory I carried stones'.

ELENA. Oh I love that...

ELENA *traces the tattoo with her fingers...*

RAGNAR. From a French poem. Except they spelled the word *pierres* wrong but whatever –

Then, ELENA *pulls him into a kiss.*

After a beat, RAGNAR *tries to delicately pull away –*

Oh no, I'm sorry I –

ELENA. No you're not –

RAGNAR. Elena –

ELENA. *Kiss me.*

> ELENA *kisses him again. As* RAGNAR *tries to evade her advances* –

RAGNAR. Elena, *please* –

> *A sound outside the doorway.*

ELENA. What was that?

RAGNAR. I don't know.

ELENA. Is someone out there?

RAGNAR. No, couldn't be –

> ELENA *stands up, and goes to the source of the sound.*
>
> *And there she finds:* KAIA. *Hiding.*

ELENA. OH MY GOD –

KAIA. It's not what you think –

ELENA. I don't need to think, I have two fucking eyes!!!

KAIA. Please, let me explain –

ELENA. DON'T YOU DARE.

RAGNAR. Elena, please wait a moment –

ELENA. You know, Kaia, I can't say I'm shocked, but I am impressed – I didn't think you had it in you to act like a *deceitful little slut.*

> KAIA *runs off in tears, and* RAGNAR *follows her.*
>
> ELENA *is left alone.*
>
> *It's dark out now, the insects buzzing madly.*
>
> ELENA *refills her whiskey and vapes, unraveling.*

(*To herself.*) I'm such an idiot, I'm such a fucking idiot –

> HILDE *enters and sees* ELENA.

(*Calling out.*) SO DID YOU DO IT?

HILDE *stops in her tracks.*

DID YOU? Did you bring Henry to his knees? Or did you just get down on your own knees instead?

Beat. They stare at each other.

HILDE. I don't want to bring him down, Elena.

ELENA. Fine, then. You've made your choice, and now I'm left to make my own.

HILDE. I'm sorry?

ELENA. Hilde, I offered to help you – to 'amplify' your voice, to 'reframe' your narrative, *whatever*. But you rejected my proposal.

HILDE. Not everything is a negotiation.

ELENA. Of course it is. A negotiation of power is no different than a negotiation of desire. <u>Someone always comes out on top.</u>

HILDE. I don't think that's true.

ELENA. Really? Let me give you another example then. Instead of offering to help sell your novel… I could do the opposite. I could instead warn the editors that your manuscript is *radioactive* – that they shouldn't go anywhere near it.

HILDE. You wouldn't do that.

ELENA. Why not?

HILDE. You wouldn't try to blackball me again…

ELENA. I could. With one *click*.

HILDE. But I didn't do anything *wrong*.

ELENA. No? Denying accountability again? You girls claim to have all this agency, all this power… but the moment you *regret* your own choices, your own mistakes, where does it all go?

HILDE. I don't regret anything…

ELENA. Then why is it *smeared* all over your pretty little face.

Beat. HILDE *stops breathing.*

Relax, my god! I'm not going to do it. You can *breathe.* Consider it a... mental exercise.

ELENA *refills two glasses.*

Here, DRINK UP!

ELENA *offers her a glass.* HILDE *uneasily accepts it.*

You know, Hilde, at the end of the day, you and I are more similar than you think.

HILDE. How so...

ELENA. We want to believe that we are strong enough to assert control over our bodies, our destinies, our cunts. We can fuck like men, climb the ranks like men. We are not victims, no, we are not frail Victorian women! I was *not* the betrayed, childless wife, and you were *not* the groomed, exploited student.

Beat.

But why are we constantly telling ourselves these... lies?

HILDE. Are they?

ELENA. You know, after my son died, I barely took time off. I was afraid if I did, I'd be replaced – by a man. So I worked even harder, numbing my grief, but it didn't matter – some wanker was still promoted to the role I deserved. And meanwhile, Henry was *rewarded* for working harder – he won international competition after competition, he joined the galaxy of starchitects! They called him 'the *rock star* of architecture' as if he was Mick fucking Jagger.

HENRY *hovers in the doorway, though he remains in the shadows. Unseen.*

It's absurd, really. Men have to do so little be worshipped, to be canonized, and women have to do so much just to be *seen.* Here I was, suffering through miscarriages and IVF injections which were replaced by hot flushes and hormone therapy... while Henry rose to the top of the fucking world!

Beat. ELENA *picks up her vape, but her hands are shaking.*

ACT TWO, SCENE FOUR 77

And it was Henry's fault to begin with. The accident... Did you know that?

HILDE. No...

ELENA. He never told you the story? In all your intimate office hours together?

HILDE *shakes her head, uncertain if she wants to hear this.*

HILDE. You don't have to tell me...

ELENA. Henry had won the commission to turn the old Whaler's Church into a contemporary art museum – after it had been left in ruins for decades. It was already in the early stages of construction, but there was community opposition – and Henry was under a lot pressure at the time. One weekend, he had to come up early for a site visit, and Max wanted to go with him... since I had to stay in the city for work, I agreed.

ELENA *now sees the image of* HENRY, *standing in the doorway. She hesitates for a moment, then continues on...*

And Max was always spooked by that old church... it looked like a run-down haunted house, curious to any little boy. Apparently, Henry assumed that Max was playing right here, in the backyard. But instead, he had run over to the church alone – he probably wanted to play architect, like his father. But the site was unsafe, all exposed wires and wood. A <u>deathtrap</u>. And Henry was distracted, he didn't notice his son was gone...

Beat.

When the fire broke out, it all went up in a blaze, ripping through the roof. And Max couldn't escape.

HILDE. I'm so sorry, Elena.

HILDE *is deeply shaken.*

HENRY *quietly retreats.*

ELENA. I'm not telling you this to elicit your sympathy. I'm telling you so that you know how *resentment* can poison the blood, like fumes from a flame... odorless, invisible. So when I found out, later that year, Henry had fallen for an undergraduate, *a junior…*

HILDE. Then why didn't you blame *him* instead of trying to ruin me?

ELENA. Because I truly loved Henry, do you understand? The only man I'd ever loved, the only man I'd wanted a *family* with – a child.

Beat. Cracking.

Until you've felt that, in the pit of your *womb*, you cannot know how far you'll go to protect whatever love remains.

Beat. ELENA *is undone by her own revelation.*

HILDE (*remorseful*). I don't know what to say. I didn't steal your husband, Elena.

ELENA. No. You just fucked him and left him for me to take care of, which is *worse*.

KAIA *tiptoes in, trying to remain unseen.*

(*Calling out.*) Oh THERE SHE IS. My loyal and trustworthy protégé! The product of female mentorship!

KAIA. I was just heading back to the party…

ELENA. You know, if we are really looking to point fingers here, if we are yielding to the *witch-huntery* of this current moment… then, Kaia, you shouldn't be totally exculpated.

KAIA. Umm…

KAIA *glances at* HILDE, *as if they are both in grave danger.*

ELENA. Think about it, Hilde. Who did you bring with you to the party that night – at my apartment? Wasn't it your best friend here, your classmate?

HILDE. Yes…

ELENA. You really never put it together? Wasn't Kaia envious that you were the object of your famous professor's desire? That Henry gave *you* an A-plus, and hired *you* for the prestigious job working for him the summer after your class…

ACT TWO, SCENE FOUR 79

HILDE *shifts, thrown by this unexpected turn.*

HILDE. So…?

ELENA. And wasn't it Kaia who saw you go into the bedroom with Henry at the party? And wasn't she the one friend who you confided in afterwards?

HILDE. What are you getting at?

ELENA. I know for a *fact* it was Kaia who sent that anonymous tip to the Dean – reporting the inappropriate student–teacher relationship between you and Henry.

Beat.

Otherwise I would never have found out.

HILDE *stares at* KAIA, *processing this betrayal.*

KAIA. Hilde…

ELENA. So if it weren't for her *treachery*, your life might've been very different. And perhaps so would mine.

Beat. KAIA *turns to face* ELENA.

KAIA. You know, I feel nothing but *pity* for you. I've watched you hide behind this platform of female empowerment, wielding it like a weapon to mask your own wounds, your own weakness. But all you want, so desperately, is the thing you fear the most: to be *loved*. To feel *worthy* of love.

Beat.

And the truth is, Elena, that's something you'll never have until you learn to forgive yourself.

Beat. As ELENA *lets this sink in…*

ELENA. I'm sorry. Excuse me –

ELENA *exits.*

KAIA *turns to* HILDE.

KAIA. I'm sorry, Hilde, I'm so sorry.

HILDE. I don't even know what to say anymore.

KAIA. You have to remember, we were barely twenty at the time, we were practically *babies* –

HILDE. I know that –

KAIA. – but I never meant to hurt you. I naively thought I was protecting you.

HILDE (*at a loss*). But I don't understand... Why did you want me to come here today? Why did *you* insist that I come?

Beat. They hold each other's hands.

KAIA. Maybe I still blame myself for what happened to you. And the only way I could make amends was to remind us of who we were back then, as girls, and to see now how far we've come.

HILDE. But have we...?

KAIA. Yes, Hilde, you *know* we have. We thought we knew so much about the world then, we believed our power was *symmetrical*. But it wasn't. We looked to these *adults* to help construct our character while it was still forming... and instead, they imprinted us with their own scars.

HENRY *comes back in.*

HENRY. Are we surviving...?

KAIA. We're in survival mode, that's for fucking sure! I'm going back to the party.

KAIA *exits.*

HENRY *and* HILDE *are left alone.*

HENRY. What's happened?

HILDE. Nothing... everything.

HENRY *tries to pull her into his arms.*

HENRY. It's all going to be okay...

HILDE. Is it?

HENRY. Yes, you're safe with me now.

HILDE *pulls away. She looks at him. Something irrevocably transformed within her.*

What is it...?

HILDE. How come you never showed up to meet me that day?

HENRY. When?

HILDE. In Riverside Park, that October...

Beat.

We hadn't seen each other since the summer... we had no contact, and I was forced to drop your independent study that semester. I was so depressed, I almost took a leave of absence from school. Did you know that?

HENRY. No...

HILDE. So finally I reached out, asking if we could talk. I was so idiotically happy when you responded... saying to meet at our spot, the Soldiers' and Sailors' Monument on 89th Street. Where we used to meet for our long evening walks...

HENRY. Yes, I remember...

HILDE. I'd been so distraught by your silence, as if I had done something wrong... So the promise of seeing you again filled me with this... glimmer of hope.

Beat.

So I went to the monument, and waited. There was a chill in the air, and I wrapped myself in your red scarf. I waited and waited till dark. But you never came...

HENRY. Oh Hilde... my Hilde...

HILDE. I'd never felt so abandoned, so *discarded* before.

Beat.

Why didn't you come?

HENRY. Elena forbid me from ever seeing you or talking to you again. She threatened to leave me if I did, and I... I was a coward, a weak, weak man. I had been so wracked with guilt for what I had done, I couldn't face it...

HILDE. I assumed it all meant nothing to you. That *I* meant nothing to you.

HENRY. No, no, it meant *everything* to me –

HILDE. But I carried around that sense of *worthlessness* for years.

HENRY. Oh god, Hilde, it *killed* me not to see you again – it nearly destroyed me too –

HILDE. But you *thrived*! I saw your name everywhere, larger than life, while I felt so insignificant.

HENRY *gets down on his knees before her, penitent and pleading.*

HENRY. Hilde, forgive me, please forgive me –

HILDE. Henry, get up –

HENRY. Please fucking forgive me. I swear, I will never let you go –

HILDE. But how can I <u>trust</u> you again, after what happened?

Beat. HILDE *has revealed her own deepest fear, and it shatters them both.*

HENRY. I promise you, <u>on my own life</u>.

HILDE. *Don't say that.*

HENRY. Hilde, for the past decade, I could only see the future through the construction of space, but I couldn't see the outline of my own life.

Beat.

And now I can again. I see the one with *you* in it.

HILDE. But it's an *illusion* –

HENRY. Don't say that. I know I've failed in so many ways, but the *one thing* I can materialize is the promise I made to you.

HILDE. And what if I don't <u>want</u> that anymore?

HENRY. I thought that's the reason you came back…?

Beat. HILDE *looks at him, wrenched, grappling to reconcile her past with her present.*

HILDE. When I came here today, part of me was still clinging to this dream we shared together. Our insoluble love that I carried like a dark secret in my heart. There were so many questions that haunted me I couldn't answer. And now I realize…

Beat.

I've been holding onto a version of myself I was scared to let go of. But I had already left her behind.

HILDE *is crying now.*

HENRY. No, no, she's right here, in front of my eyes. The same girl who walked into my classroom on a cold January. The same girl who showed me there's infinite possibility, even when you believe that life has none left to offer.

HENRY *kisses her.*

As ELENA *re-enters, bounding back in.*

ELENA. Sorry.

Beat.

Did I interrupt your little lovers' quarrel? Has the post-coital haze worn off already?

HENRY (*coldly*). What do you want.

ELENA. You know, you two look good together, really you do. Doesn't give off the whiff of middle-age crisis at all!

HENRY. STOP IT.

ELENA. No, I'm serious. You've always wanted another child, so why not explore more fertile pastures? It's only *biological* –

HENRY *protectively shields* HILDE.

HENRY (*to* HILDE). You don't have to listen to this –

ELENA. I mean, I can just imagine you at kindergarten drop-off – I'm sure she'd love to call you Daddy.

HENRY. *I'm warning you, Elena –*

ELENA. But then one day, my darling girl, you'll grow tired of him, the power differential will no longer be erotic but *exhausting*, and you'll resent the years he's stolen from you – and you will suddenly realize that your youth was wasted on a broken old man.

HENRY (*shouting*). ENOUGH!!!

HILDE. I'm sorry –

Wrecked, HILDE *flees the scene.*

HENRY *turns to face* ELENA. *His breaking point reached.*

ELENA. Why don't you run after her? Cause a dramatic scene.

HENRY. Shall I? Is that what you want?

ELENA. If you want to make a *fool* of yourself, be my guest.

HENRY. Oh I think you've already done that – you've already won the fucking crown. If that's been your goal, then BRAVO!

ELENA. That was *not* my goal.

HENRY. Then what was it? To relentlessly *punish* me?

ELENA. No...

HENRY. Because I think I have done my fair fucking share. Every single day for ten years, *suffering* for my sins to give you the *satisfaction* that my guilt was not for nothing. So long as I was the one who had something to feel guilty about – and not you.

ELENA. That's not true –

HENRY. No? Then why did you invite her here today? TELL ME WHY.

ELENA. I don't know... I don't know...

HENRY. You bloody well know! It was a fucking self-fulfilling prophecy!

ELENA. No no no no no –

HENRY. You accused me of betraying you when we were *separated*, you held it over my head because it was *easier* than blaming me for his death… which I know you do every day. *I know*.

ELENA. No more than I blame myself.

HENRY. Well now you got what you wanted. I finally <u>fucked</u> her. Are you happy now?

ELENA. Yes, thrilled.

HENRY. Do you feel vindicated?

ELENA. Can't you tell.

> HENRY *is gaining momentum, the unflinching truth releasing a reserve of power within him.*

HENRY. And you know what I can't understand… all these years you *pushed* me to leave you – you cheated on me again and again, you didn't even bother to hide it. And I said *nothing*! Like some pathetic fucking chump.

ELENA (*crying out*). I only did it so you would CARE – about anything other than steel and stone! I wanted you to care about <u>me</u>.

HENRY. Of course I *cared* –

ELENA. Then why didn't you even *ask* me about it?

HENRY. I didn't have to ask because everyone was talking about it – it was impossible *not* to know!

ELENA. But you didn't *care* enough to know if it was true?

HENRY. Why would I want to know that?

ELENA. Because you're my <u>husband</u>! But you weren't even bothered – all I wanted, Henry, was to make you jealous, to make you *want* me again, to make you feel <u>any emotion at all</u>!

HENRY. WELL NOW I FEEL ALL OF THEM!!!

> HENRY *erupts. He picks up a plate from the table and throws it.*

PASSION! PAIN! DESIRE! DESPAIR!

> *Exhilarated by his own discharged emotion,* HENRY *throws more plates until the table is nearly destroyed.*

I FEEL EVERY FUCKING FEELING I HAVEN'T FELT IN YEARS!!!

ELENA. Jesus Christ, Henry, stop it – !!

HENRY. And you want to know why? Because I'm a <u>free man</u> now, the shackles of guilt have been unchained. It took a woman capable of *love* in her heart to remind me that I deserve to feel the same.

ELENA (*aghast*). *Love?* You think she loves you?

HENRY. Why is that so hard to believe?

ELENA. Have you lost your mind??

HENRY. If that's what it takes to realize this is <u>dead</u>, then maybe it's the sanest I've been in years.

ELENA goes to him, utterly devastated.

ELENA. It hasn't died, Henry. <u>I love you.</u>

HENRY. No, you got what you asked for. If you push someone far enough to the edge, they will finally lose their footing.

In an act of excruciating desperation, ELENA flings herself onto HENRY, weeping, trying to kiss him, to hold onto him.

ELENA. I only did it because <u>I love you</u>, I still do, I've only ever loved you. Don't you know that? I just needed to know that there was some *fight* in you left –

HENRY. Not for this, not anymore –

HENRY tries to pry her off him, but ELENA persists, pleading with him.

ELENA. Henry, I'm sorry, please forgive me –

HENRY. No, I lay down my arms –

ELENA. Let's just go back, forget this night even happened!

Finally, HENRY pulls ELENA into his arms in a heart-wrenching embrace. They cling to and hold each other for an unbearable moment.

HENRY. I believed all this time we could restore and rebuild the ruins of our life together, after a bomb had blown it to bits. But now I see… the home we have built has become uninhabitable. *A deathtrap.*

ELENA. Don't you love me anymore?

HENRY. Does it matter now?

ELENA. Yes, yes, it's the *only* thing that matters.

Beat. HENRY *takes her face in his hands, with a tragic tenderness that shatters her.*

HENRY. I've always loved you, Elena. But now I need the kind of love that contains more light than darkness.

HENRY *exits.*

Scene Five

The party. In front of the CHAPEL. (*As in Act Two, Scene One.*)

It's almost midnight now. The mood feels more hedonistic and wild, like anything can happen…

HENRY *enters, burning with febrile, manic energy. He charges over to* HILDE.

HENRY. Hilde, it's done! It's over!

HILDE. What?

HENRY. My marriage, my former life – it's all behind me now!

HILDE. Henry, calm down –

HENRY. The only way it makes sense, all these years of suffering apart, is that we can finally be *together* –

HILDE. You need to take a breath – !

HENRY (*imploring*). No, listen to me, just listen –

HILDE. Okay, okay, I'm *listening.*

Beat.

HENRY. Do you remember the party, ten years ago?

HILDE. Yes –

HENRY. How you kissed me –

HILDE. Yes, yes –

HENRY. And I held you in my arms, never wanting to let go.

HILDE. I remember.

HENRY. And I promised you, Hilde, that if you came back to me, then I would climb to the greatest heights to be with you. Didn't I promise you that?

HILDE (*nodding*). Yes, you did.

HENRY. I'm a man of my word, Hilde.

> HENRY *kisses her, and she kisses him back.*

And I'm going to prove it to you once more!

> *Suddenly,* HENRY *runs over and leaps onto the* CHAPEL.
>
> *He begins to climb. And climb.*

HILDE (*calling out*). HENRY –

HENRY. Hilde, you will see!

HILDE. HENRY!!

> HILDE *runs after* HENRY. RAGNAR *and* KAIA *notice* HENRY *scaling the* CHAPEL.

KAIA. What's he doing – ???

RAGNAR. Oh shit!

> HILDE *tries to climb the* CHAPEL *after* HENRY, *frantically calling his name. But* RAGNAR *restrains her and pulls her back down.*

HILDE. HENRY! HENRY, COME DOWN!!

> ELENA *enters, registering the commotion.*

ELENA. What's going on?

ACT TWO, SCENE FIVE 89

She looks up, and gasps. Cries out.

(*Terrified.*) What in god's name is he doing??!

RAGNAR. It's unclear.

ELENA (*calling out*). Henry. HENRY!!!

RAGNAR. Should we try get him down – ??

KAIA. YES but how?

ELENA *turns to* HILDE, *accusingly.*

ELENA. Did <u>you</u> tell him to do this??

HILDE. No, of course not!

ELENA (*panicking*). Ragnar, do something – tell him to come down! He shouldn't be up there, with his vertigo –

RAGNAR. HENRY!!! Come on down, buddy! Come on, boss!

HENRY *has now nearly reached the peak of the* CHAPEL. *As if he is ascending into some higher realm.*

HENRY. From up here, I can see everything. The stretch of sea. The stars. The vanishing point on the horizon. I see how small our lives are. All this time, I believed these buildings would outlast me, they would remain a part of history long after we perished. But now I see... what endures, in the end, is beyond glass and steel and stone...

Beat. Looking down towards the earth.

The only thing that will endure of us is love.

A burst of fireworks suddenly illuminates the night sky.

HENRY *shields his eyes from the blinding light.*

ELENA (*shrieking*). Oh god the fireworks – !

ELENA *runs off.*

HENRY *looks down, desperately trying to locate* HILDE *below. He grabs onto the* CHAPEL *to steady himself.*

HENRY (*calling out*). Hilde! Hilde, where are you??

HILDE. I'm right here!

> HILDE *jumps up and down, screaming over the booming fireworks.*

HENRY. Where??

HILDE. HERE! I'm here!

> *The fireworks intensify in light and sound. The* CHAPEL *reflects and refracts the dazzling colors: fiery orange to neon-pink to blood-red.*

> HENRY *feels the colors exploding inside of his head, triggering his vertigo. He becomes disoriented, sky and sea inverted. For a moment, he loses his balance.*

> *But the* GUESTS *are now watching the fireworks.*

> *Only* HILDE *is left, shaking, looking up at the* CHAPEL. *Until* HENRY *is no longer in view.*

> *After a thunderous finale, the fireworks stop.*

> *Then: the sound of* ELENA*'s harrowing scream pierces through the night.*

> HENRY *is lying unconscious on the ground.*

> *And* HILDE *is gone.*

ELENA. HENRY!! HENRY!!!

> ELENA *runs over to* HENRY, *sobbing and screaming his name, throwing her body over his.*

KAIA. Oh my god I can't look –

RAGNAR. Fuck –

KAIA. We've got to call an ambulance!

RAGNAR (*on his phone*). I'm trying!

KAIA. Do you think he's – ?

RAGNAR. No, it's not that far of a fall, I'm sure he's fine, everything will be alright –

ELENA *is now cradling and rocking* HENRY *in her arms, kissing his face.*

ELENA. It's okay, you're going to be okay –

HENRY*'s eyes flicker open.*

OH HENRY THANK GOODNESS!

HENRY (*weakly*). What's happened?

ELENA. Nothing, you took a little fall. Just stay with me, Henry, stay with me, I'm right here –

As HENRY *regains consciousness, everything dims in his vision…*

He reaches out his hand into the dark.

HENRY. My – Hilde.

HILDE *slowly appears on the horizon. A halo of light shining around her.*

ELENA *looks up at her.* HILDE *holds her gaze.*

As the waves crash against the shore, HILDE *fades into the distance.*

Blackout.

MARKETSTALL

Marketstall is a UK-based production company established by John Brant in 2023, producing work nationally and internationally.

Theatre includes: *Macbeth* with Ralph Fiennes and Indira Varma (Liverpool, Edinburgh, London, Washington DC) and *The Enfield Haunting* with Catherine Tate and David Threlfall (Ambassadors Theatre).

MGC

MGC is a London-based company that produces work across all media, nationally and internationally. The company also provides a General Management service to other producers and represents a select group of creative practitioners.

MGC productions include: *Backstairs Billy* with Penelope Wilton and Luke Evans; *Orlando* with Emma Corrin; *Dawn French is a Huge Tw*t*, and *The Lemon Table* with Ian McDiarmid (UK Tour).

Also in the West End: *The Lieutenant of Inishmore* with Aidan Turner; *Red* with Alfred Molina and Alfred Enoch; *Labour of Love* (co-produced with Headlong) with Martin Freeman and Tamsin Greig; *Photograph 51* with Nicole Kidman; *Henry V* with Jude Law; *A Midsummer Night's Dream* with David Walliams and Sheridan Smith; *The Cripple of Inishmaan* with Daniel Radcliffe (and on Broadway); *Peter and Alice* with Judi Dench and Ben Whishaw; *Privates on Parade* with Simon Russell Beale; and *Hughie* on Broadway with Forest Whitaker.

MGC co-produced (with Emily Dobbs Productions) *The Dazzle* with Andrew Scott, and Dawn French's *30 Million Minutes* (with Phil McIntyre Entertainment) in the West End, and on tour in the UK and internationally. MGC previously general managed *School of Rock – The Musical* at the Gillian Lynne Theatre, and the 20th Anniversary production of *Rent* at the St James Theatre and on tour.

The company produced the feature film *My Policeman* (2022) starring Harry Styles, Emma Corrin, Gina McKee, Linus Roache, David Dawson and Rupert Everett which had its world premiere at Toronto International Film Festival. They also produced *Genius* (2016) starring Colin Firth, Jude Law, Nicole Kidman, and Laura Linney which premiered at the Berlin Film Festival. Both films were directed by Michael Grandage. michaelgrandagecompany.com

seaview

Seaview is a Tony, Olivier and Peabody Award-winning theatre and film company. This season: *Romeo and Juliet*, *Hold On To Me Darling*, *All In: Comedy About Love*, *Good Night, and Good Luck; The Last Five Years* and *Once Upon a Mattress*.

Past credits include: *Reality* (HBO); *Stress Positions* (NEON); the Tony Award-winning *Stereophonic;* Sam Gold's *An Enemy of the People* starring Jeremy Strong; Justin Peck and Jackie Sibblies Drury's *Illinois*; *Lempicka* directed by Rachel Chavkin; Michael Arden's Tony Award-winning revival of *Parade*; Alex Edelman's Emmy Award-winning *Just For Us*; Lorraine Hansberry's *The Sign In Sidney Brustein's Window*; Mike Birbiglia's *The Old Man & The Pool*; Selina Fillinger's *POTUS*; Jeremy O. Harris' *Slave Play*; *Sea Wall / A Life* starring Jake Gyllenhaal and Tom Sturridge; and *Sweeney Todd* at the Barrow Street Theatre.

Upcoming: *Angry Alan* starring John Krasinski; and *The Queen of Versailles* starring Kristin Chenoweth.

Seaview also operates Studio Seaview, a 296-seat Off Broadway Theatre located at 305 West 43rd. @ThisIsSeaview @StudioSeaview

www.nickhernbooks.co.uk

@nickhernbooks